The Node Book

Zipporah Pottenger Dobyns, Ph.D.

ISBN-10: 0-86690-606-1
ISBN-13: 978-0-86690-606-7

Cover Design: Jack Cipolla
Computer Programming: Mark Pottenger and Rique Pottenger

Published by:
American Federation of Astrologers, Inc.
6535 S. Rural Road
Tempe, AZ 85283

www.astrologers.com

Printed in the United States of America

The great gift of air is perspective. We put space between ourselves and something else so that we can see the whole picture. Humanity's venture into space in the 1960s gave us the thrill of seeing our Earth in this way. For thousands of years astrology has been humanity's way to see the whole cosmic order. The sky does not create the order but it *is* the order spread out there before our eyes if we have the wisdom to understand the complicated cycles. Air symbolizes the conscious, reasoning mind that can see, understand, and deal rationally with the panoramic, evolving view.

Contents

Chapter 1, Philosophizing   1
Chapter 2, General Principles   5
Chapter 3, Planetary Nodes   11
    Mercury   11
    Venus   14
    Mars   16
    Jupiter   18
    Saturn   21
    Uranus   24
    Neptune   26
    Pluto   27
    The Asteroids   30
Chapter 4, Nodes of the Moon   39
    Aries-Libra or First House-Seventh House   41
    Taurus-Scorpio or Second House-Eighth House   43
    Gemini-Sagittarius or Third House-Ninth House   45
    Cancer-Capricorn or Fourth House-Tenth House   47
    Leo-Aquarius or Fifth House-Eleventh House   49
    Virgo-Pisces or Sixth House-Twelfth House   50
Chapter 5, Summing Up   53
Node Tables for Planets   55
Node Tables for Asteroids   91

Foreword

This volume is offered with the hope that it will be useful in broadening the horizons and also in clarifying the principles associated with astrology. The series is designed to provide additional tools for serious students of this ancient art, especially for those who will undertake the task of validating the correspondences between the affairs of Earth and the patterns in the solar system and beyond. To accomplish such a task, and to attain a synthesis of validated scientific principles and intuitive art, modern research techniques must be applied to the problem and all possible astrological factors must be available for testing.

This series will offer new or little known factors, which may prove of value in astrological interpretation. Since little scientifically acceptable research is yet available, all statements on astrological principles in this series are to be considered hypotheses to be tested. Examples given should be considered suggestive only, since it is not possible to give full chart interpretations in the available space.

As this volume goes into its fifth printing, there is evidence for the importance of both geocentric and heliocentric positions of the nodes. New techniques of multivariate analysis are being applied to astrological data with encouraging results. One study of hemophilia suggests that certain aspects between geocentric planetary nodes and the heliocentric positions of the planets as well as aspects of geocentric nodes to geocentric positions of the planets distinguish the subject group from a control group. Much additional work is needed to replicate and extend the findings but the importance of the nodes has been strongly supported. The fact that an interaction between geocentric and heliocentric positions seems validated by this ongoing research also supports the nonmaterial nature of astrology. The differing viewpoints of Earth and Sun are particularly striking for the inner planets, Mercury, and Venus and their nodes. Mercury in 19 degrees of Scorpio as seen from the Sun would be in a totally different place in the sky from Venus in 19 degrees of Scorpio as seen from Earth. If there is a correspondence between them, it suggests that the zodiac is an abstract key to meaning rather than an area in space of energy fields or material force. As is usual, the more we search for answers the more we discover new questions.

Zipporah Pottenger Dobyns

Chapter 1

Philosophizing

HUMANITY'S SEARCH for knowledge is increasingly recognized as one of the motivating dynamics of life, partly driven by the need to predict and control the world for security, but also partly as a source of personal satisfaction, as an end in itself. The discovery that the patterns observed in the sky somehow corresponded to events occurring on Earth was apparently made early in history. Astrology was a recognized and revered study by the time writing was developed, and it is found in every area of Earth advanced enough to have attained a civilization which included writing. The fact of such correspondences becomes quickly obvious to any serious student of the subject. To tell someone who has investigated astrology in depth that "astrology is a myth" is equivalent to telling someone who has just fallen down stairs that "gravity is a myth." But the reasons for the correspondences are neither obvious nor easy to substantiate.

At present, the whole philosophy of science is under scrutiny and many entrenched theories and methods are being challenged. Although scientists may still be encountered who would assert, like Gertrude Stein, that "a fact is a fact is a fact," the philosophers of science point out that it is not possible to even define a "fact" without the context of a theory. Until a theory is present, there is only a flowing stream of sensations. The theory identifies which of these sensations are real versus illusory according to your theoretical nature of reality; it indicates which are true, meaningful, and important now or with portent for the future; and it indicates which are morally good or tainted regardless or any immediate pleasure to be derived from the sensation. Still more importantly, it is only in recent years that such philosophers of science have acknowledged that even the most tightly reasoned and empirically supported theories rest ultimately on postulates or assumptions that cannot be proven. The absolutes, final reality, truth, and moral goodness, are not susceptible to the partial proofs of empirical method. They are articles of faith.

Since it is impossible to have a science that does not rest on faith or a faith that is unsupported by some evidence, however inadequate, the issue is no longer factual science versus religious or intuitive faith, but *which faith* supported by *which evidence?*

This recognition of the theoretical nature of all worldviews, including the scientific one, opens up a whole new chapter in the human search for meaning and direction in life. Humanity can move again toward a synthesis of theology, philosophy, and psychology such as the ancient world attained, and do so with vastly increased knowledge due to the addition of modern instruments and methods, including the techniques of modern mathematics. Whether we do or do not believe in a personal deity who geometrizes, or whether we are upset at the suggestion that God plays dice with the universe (Einstein's reaction to modern probability theory), we must acknowledge the invaluable role played by mathematics in the scientific search for truth. Mathematics provides science with a universal language with which to describe or represent reality in order to handle it conceptually. Anything that can be counted or measured can be described with this language of numbers.

It is suggested here that, until we have further evidence on the reasons for, or mechanisms that may lie behind the fact of astrological correspondences, we consider astrology as a second language to describe reality—a qualitative one to place beside the quantitative one of mathematics, though the latter is also becoming qualitative in recent years. Both use systems of symbols, but the language of astrology describes the universe in psychological, philosophical, and spiritual terms, offering these as the central realities lying behind the specific events of a given life. In the earliest groping for reasons that explained the pragmatically observed correspondences between planetary patterns and Earth events, humans theorized that a God occupied or directed planetary motion and the Earth consequences. The few scientists that have dared to investigate this heretical field have operated within the materialistic belief system and have offered force fields to account for the correspondences. Both theories consider the planets to be the cause, with the events on Earth accepted as consequences. It is suggested that, until we have much more evidence, it is wiser to postpone such an assumption, to leave open the possibility that a larger, unifying cause lies behind both the planetary movements and the unfolding of life on Earth.

As humans, we need a faith by which to live. We have to believe in something in order to rank values, set goals, and make daily choices. We may reach this faith through mystical visions, through complicated superstructures of reason and logic based on postulates appropriate to the culture of the day, or through the pragmatic methods of action and feedback endorsed in modern science, but in the end we seek a monistic simplicity, a unifying central reality, and cannot be satisfied with less. Though there is no real justification for the faith in such a monistic world-view when we look at the chaos of life on Earth, the gravitation toward it is so strong that we must consider it either an instinct for a far-from obvious truth and/or as a desperate need for a security which is unobtainable in a chaotic world. The modern studies of alienation, anomie, and the "existential vacuum" point up the anguish of life without such a worldview and sense of meaningfulness.

The primary rival worldviews today are the materialistic versus the idealistic ones, with, of course, numerous sub-variants of each. Modern science has, until very recently, been grounded in the first, reducing all existence to primary energy charges in constant motion. The energy charges are said to follow the laws of their nature in a meaningless, purposeless world, likened to a giant machine that is gradually running down. Most humans through most of recorded history have believed in one of the sub-variants of the idealistic worldview, whether they called it theism, deism, pantheism, or spiritualism. In this view, the primary reality is consciousness in an evolving world, which is like a giant mind experimenting, manifesting latent potentials of ever increasing complexity. While some variations put the creative force (God or Spirit) outside of and separate from the material world, and some put it in, they agree that life is meaningful, purposeful, and continuous beyond the present world of the material senses.

The individual's choice among these variant metaphysical systems, including the scientific one, is inevitably influenced by early conditioning, emotional needs, intellectual capacity, and contact with alternative views. The raw data of astrology, the correspondences between events of Earth and patterns in the sky, can be interpreted within the framework of any of them, and has been interpreted by such spokesmen as St. Thomas Aquinas, writing within the tenets of the Catholic Church; John Nelson, using the theories of materialistic force fields in his prediction of ionospheric disturbances; Carl Jung, avoiding the question of cause with the concept of synchronicity; and occultists, suggesting that karma brings a baby back to a pattern that fits the nature created in a past life rather than the accident of birth being responsible for the personality and character and the destiny that will flow from them. It is hoped that, whatever your belief system, you will find something of value in this work to aid you in the search for meaning and truth.

Chapter 2

General Principles

ASTRONOMICALLY, THE word "node" refers to the point at which a planet crosses the extended plane of another planet's orbit. For example, if we extend the plane of the Earth's orbit (or path around the Sun) to the point of intersection with the Moon's orbit (or path around the Earth), we obtain the nodes of the Moon. At the north node, the Moon crosses the Earth's orbital plane in its movement into north celestial latitude. The Moon crosses the plane of the ecliptic back into south celestial latitude at the south node. The nodes of the planets also mark the points at which their respective orbits intersect the extension of the Earth's orbit, the ecliptic, their north node marking their entry into north celestial latitude and the south node the return to south latitude.

Just as it is possible to obtain both geocentric (Earth-centered) and heliocentric (Sun-centered) positions for the planets, it is possible to give the nodes of the planets in both systems of reference. Use of the geocentric frame of reference does not imply a belief that the Earth is the center of the universe. Reality may be studied from any reference point and the results will be related to the place of observation as well as to the methods used and the state of the observer. In the end, the relative value of differing systems must be judged by pragmatic results.

Instead of thinking of the nodes as points where a planetary orbit crosses the plane of Earth's orbit, it is also possible to think of the intersection of the planes of both orbits to produce a "line of nodes." If this line is extended to infinity, the geocentric and heliocentric positions of the nodes are the same since the viewpoint of Earth and Sun are relatively close when observing very distant objects. This effect can be noted for Pluto and Neptune; their geocentric nodes are never far from their heliocentric positions. Initial work with these still little-known and used factors suggests that both heliocentric and geocentric positions may be useful in our normal geocentric charts.

The nodes of the Moon used by most astrologers, and the nodes of the planets presented here, are *mean nodes*. Mean nodes are the intersections of the average orbits of other bodies with the plane of the Earth's orbit. The motion of mean nodes is even and predictable from simple formulae. *osculating nodes* for the planets can be derived from their positions at any given moment. The osculating elements (node, perihelion, etc.) describe the orbit of the planet as determined from its position at a specific moment. Osculating elements vary unpredictably—there is no simple formula for getting their positions. To get the osculating elements for any given time you must know the planets' positions. The true node of the Moon is much like the osculating nodes of the planets; it is based on the Moon's position from moment to moment rather than a mean orbit. To use the osculating nodes of the planets or the true node of the Moon, you need a daily ephemeris for all the years you are interested in.

This book gives the geocentric positions of the mean planetary nodes for one full year, with the change in position during a century to allow correction for the motion of the heliocentric nodes. Directions on how to use the tables precede them. The nodes for Mercury through Neptune are mean nodes to be found in the *Explanatory Supplement* to the *Astronomical Ephemeris* and the *American Ephemeris* and *Nautical Almanac*. The node for Pluto was derived by James Neely of Carmel and published in *Matrix Two*. The nodes for the asteroids were derived by Mark Pottenger for this book. The Pluto and asteroid nodes are a least squares fit to a series of osculating nodes derived from planetary positions. They are thus averaged osculating nodes. They had to be derived because we couldn't find mean nodes published for Pluto or the asteroids in the available astronomical literature. The asteroid nodes might be slightly less accurate than the others because the asteroid positions they are derived from are only accurate to two decimal places and the formulae to get the osculating elements are extremely sensitive. The elements were derived at twenty-day intervals for most of a century, so the averaging should have smoothed out any errors to get reasonably good positions.

Tradition states that the north node symbolizes an area of intake where matters flow with relative ease. The South node, in contrast, appears to be a point of release or outflow, often with an accompanying sense of stress or tension or pressure.

Tradition as well as personal work also suggests that the qualities of the respective planets, or of the Moon, are associated with their nodal positions, and these will be considered in more detail in later chapters. If we accept the occult view that we are born at a time when our horoscope fits and describes the tendencies, talents and weaknesses that we have developed in past lives, the north node may represent matters already learned where we can continue to function with minimal strain, while the south node indicates an area where we must put forth effort—first to learn the needed lesson and then to give to the world the fruits of our learning. In every case, it is necessary to consider sign and house position as well as aspects to other features of the chart before making our judgment.

The nodes of the Moon and the heliocentric nodes of the planets are always opposite each other, and as is usual with an opposition, they represent a natural partnership of principles that are complementary to each other and which need to be integrated as a functioning team. If they are not so integrated, the individual may repress one side of the opposition or may project it and find others to act it out, or the individual may swing like a pendulum between the respective poles. The heliocentric positions of the planetary nodes may be important when other features in the chart (i.e., planets, angles, etc.) aspect them. The Moon's nodes (sign and house position) seem important in their own right as keys to talents and to problems, regardless of aspects, but their weight is, of course, increased if there are strong natal or progressed aspects to them. The geocentric positions of the planetary nodes have been under observation for too short a time to make definitive statements about them, but they also seem to operate as keys to personal matters with the personal planets Mercury: Venus and Mars. From Jupiter out, aspects to other features of the chart seem necessary to show significance in the sign positions of the nodes, but such aspects turn up with high frequency in the charts of world figures. Indeed it is somewhat rare to find such a person who lacks a planet or angle in the area of 18 to 25 degrees of the cardinal signs where the nodes of Pluto, Saturn and often Jupiter appear. House positions of the geocentric nodes of all planets may be significant.

The geocentric north and south nodes of the inner planets, Mercury and Venus, may appear in any zodiacal sign. The nodes of Mercury can range from a conjunction when they are lined up with the Sun twice a year at 17 degrees of Taurus and Scorpio, on the north and south heliocentric nodes, to a maximum separation of about 45 degrees. The Venus nodes similarly line up with the Sun at 16 degrees of Gemini and Sagittarius, on the heliocentric positions, and their maximum separation is about a quintile of 72 degrees. The geocentric nodes of Mars range from about 7 Aries to 2 Cancer for the north node and about 8 Libra to 29 Sagittarius for the south node. As the distance from the Sun increases, the viewpoints of Sun and Earth converge so that the geocentric nodes remain within smaller arcs until, with Pluto, there is little difference between the geocentric and the heliocentric positions. For the sign areas covered by the other planetary nodes, see Table 1.

Testing so far has been mostly focused on the natal positions of the nodes, watching for ways in which they indicate personality factors, but evidence is accumulating to support the value of progressed aspects and transits touching natal nodes, and of pro-

Table 1. 1950 Ranges of Geocentric Nodes

		Minimum	*Maximum*	*Range*
♂	NN	07 ♈ 17	02 ♋ 06	84°49′
	SN	08 ♎ 12	29 ♐ 09	80 57
⚳	NN	29 ♉ 6	12 ♋ 37	43 31
	SN	29 ♏ 44	11 ♑ 28	41 44
⚴	NN	26 ♌ 38	18 ♎ 38	52 00
	SN	04 ♓ 21	12 ♈ 17	37 56
⚵	NN	29 ♌ 06	11 ♎ 10	42 04
	SN	24 ♒ 31	17 ♈ 11	52 40
⚶	NN	20 ♊ 48	06 ♌ 55	46 07
	SN	16 ♐ 18	11 ♒ 28	55 10
♃	NN	28 ♊ 51	21 ♋ 04	22 13
	SN	28 ♐ 50	21 ♑ 03	22 13
♄	NN	16 ♋ 52	29 ♋ 33	12 41
	SN	17 ♑ 31	28 ♑ 58	11 27
♅	NN	10 ♊ 48	16 ♊ 45	05 57
	SN	10 ♐ 43	16 ♐ 44	06 01
♆	NN	09 ♌ 19	13 ♌ 08	03 49
	SN	09 ♒ 21	13 ♒ 09	03 48
♇	NN	18 ♋ 14	21 ♋ 02	02 48
	SN	17 ♑ 57	21 ♑ 20	03 23

gressed positions of the nodes. There is also evidence for the importance of aspects between the nodes of one individual and the planets, angles, or other features in the charts of other people in his/her life. In some cases, the geocentric positions of the nodes of Venus and Mars have helped to explain strong attractions and frictions between two individuals: Uranus may show a galvanizing effect, and Saturn may indicate a sense of pressure or debt, etc.

It is important to remember that no feature in astrology should be taken out of context. Among the new factors being explored in the research work at CCRS, in other centers in the United States, and in Europe, are the geocentric nodes of the planets, the distance values of the planets (see No. 2 in the TIA series on research in astrology) and midpoints between the planets. Ancient traditions being tested include dwads, Arabic parts, fixed stars, etc., but all need to be placed in the context of the whole chart. If there is a cardinal rule in astrology, it involves this principle. No feature can stand alone, and anything important will be indicated repeatedly in the chart. Preliminary results with the new tools strongly suggest that they will provide added focus and clarity, added emphasis and impact, added subtle coloring or reinforcement of qualities shown in more traditional ways. But if they do provide such added focus, emphasis, and clarity, they are well worth including in our repertoire of basic factors, and the only way we will know whether or not they are helpful is to test them. In the end, astrology is a pragmatic study. It either works or it is worthless. This booklet is offered to help serious students to find out for themselves whether or not the geocentric nodes of the planets are worth including in the astrological tool kit. Ongoing work increasingly supports the view that exact aspects of nodes to planets and angles may often mark the difference between a relatively average person with an average life, and a person with outstanding talent or problems who has an impact on the world.

For brevity, in the following chapters, the nodes will be called South Mars (for the south node of Mars), North Mercury (for the north node of Mercury), etc. References are always to geocentric positions unless heliocentric is specified, but the heliocentric positions have been included in the tables to permit testing of both positions.

Chapter 3

Planetary Nodes

Mercury

As might be predicted from the nature of Mercury, its geocentric nodes offer insights to intellectual functioning, both basic capacity and the importance of study or communication to the individual. It is possible that they also relate to travel, but this has not been tested to date. An individual may show an intense focus in the area of mental functions, whether the focus is positive or negative, when the nodes are prominent through exact aspects to planets, angles, and so on. For example, the popular singer, Donovan, has both the South and the north node of Mercury conjunct his Sun in Taurus, sextile Saturn in Cancer, and quincunx Jupiter in Libra. This emphasis on the Venus-ruled signs, Taurus and Libra, and the sign of the public and especially of females (Cancer), is an added clue to the central role of singing in his life. Singing is a form of communication especially appropriate for Taurus, which is said to rule the throat and to symbolize artistic talent and pleasure through the physical senses.

In a birth defect case, a female child born virtually without a brain had an exact square between Mercury and Uranus, keys to intelligence, which was exactly aspected by the south node of Mercury and the north nodes of Venus and Jupiter. The latter opposed Mercury from the sixth (health) house to the twelfth (house of hospitals) and was square Uranus in the house of the higher mind (ninth). All cases cited are exact within one degree for node aspects, but planetary orbs may be wider. This baby also had south Saturn and South Pluto exactly on the Ascendant, suggesting the finality and irreversible nature of the case. There are additional node aspects, another serious one being South Mars exactly conjunct Neptune in the tenth house.

On the positive side again, Einstein, one of the most remarkable minds of our time, had South Mercury conjunct his natal Jupiter in Aquarius in the ninth house while North Mercury was just beyond the one-degree orb of his natal Saturn-Mercury conjunction in Aries in the tenth house. Progressed Saturn remained conjunct North Mercury for years in his early life.

The famous occult philosopher, writer, and mystic, Krishnamurti, has both North Mercury and North Mars exactly conjunct his Sun, and his South Mercury is only two degrees away. Another well-known philosopher-writer, Alan Watts, had South Mercury in Sagittarius opposite his Saturn in Gemini, suggesting depth of mind and scholarship but also tensions involving beliefs, which is appropriate for an Anglican minister who became a famous spokesman for Eastern thought. South Jupiter conjunct Mars and south Neptune conjunct Uranus add to the religious ferment.

Former Baptist minister, Paul Solomon, who became a modern Edgar Cayce for a time and then the head of a New Age community in Virginia, has North Neptune and South Mercury conjunct natal Mercury in Leo in the twelfth house. He also has South Venus on his Ascendant and the nodes of Vesta across his natal Sun. Billy Graham, who has stayed in the Baptist fold, came in with natal Sun just between the two Mercury nodes in Scorpio in the seventh house. The south node is within the one degree orb and the north node just outside it, but the midpoint situation probably justifies our acceptance of the combination as a triple conjunction. He also has South Venus on natal Mercury in late Scorpio while North Mars is opposite it and the whole combination is exactly square Saturn in Leo in the fifth house. Another variety of missionary, the militant atheist Madalyn O'Hara, has North Mercury conjunct natal Mars in Aries in the eleventh house, among other node contacts. I call the Mercury-Mars combinations the "mind of the debater and tongue like a sword," and she is noted for her abrasive impact on people. As a supporting clue to a more broad and psychic mind, Uri Geller has South Mercury and South Uranus conjunct each other and the Antivertex. I read the latter as an auxiliary Ascendant.

Many well-known psychotherapists have close aspects to the Mercury nodes, including Sigmund Freud, the father of psychoanalysis who was born with both nodes of Mercury conjunct the Sun at 16 Taurus. He also had North Venus conjunct natal Mercury in late Taurus; all in the seventh house. Elizabeth Kubler-Ross, famous for her work on dying and her openness to the psychic area, has North Mercury conjunct natal Moon in Cancer in the fifth house, while South Mercury is conjunct natal Mercury in Leo in the sixth house. Carl Jung had North Mercury on natal Venus and North Venus on natal Mercury, a combination that should be productive of prolific writing ability and facility of speech. Fritz Perls, founder of Gestalt psychotherapy, had South Mercury on natal Mercury and North Mercury and North Venus conjunct each other and sextile natal Moon. Additional node aspects to planets include North Mars, North Jupiter, South Uranus, and both North and South Saturn and Neptune, giving us a hint of his impact on modern humanistic psychotherapy.

Timothy Leary, who had his own brand of impact as high priest of the LSD movement, had progressed South Moon conjunct South Mercury for years in addition to many other nodes aspects. The south node drive to express outwardly was evident in his life, but the stress was also present plus the implication of lessons to be learned. The Mercury-Moon contacts, even when they are between nodes rather than between the planets, seem to indicate the integration of conscious and subconscious mind which produces a popular teacher or writer, an individual with above-average intuition and interest in psychic areas, and one who will have an impact on the public through mental activity. The proselytizing urge also appears with strong aspects to the Jupiter and Neptune nodes.

Venus

Aspects to the nodes of Venus turn up frequently in individuals involved in artistic work and in cases in which love or partnership is important. Where the north node of Venus is prominent, there may be special talent. That is the case with Joan Baez who has North Venus sextile Jupiter and aspecting the nodes of the Moon, in addition to South Venus square the nodes of the Moon. There may also be a special sweetness in the nature, as in the case of a minister with North Venus on his Sun, and sometimes an exceptional devotion to suffering humanity as in the case of Martin Luther King, Jr. whose North Venus was on his natal Venus in Pisces in the eleventh house. As indicated in the chapter on general principles, the exact aspects from the nodes may not add new knowledge so much as they emphasize significant features in the chart and show the added emphasis that lifts a life into some kind of power or prominence whether the consequences are negative or positive.

South Venus has been found to be activated by aspects in individuals who were afraid to love for fear of being hurt in some way or who loved too much and suffered as a consequence, or who hungered for love and never found it. Another example of the way in which the nodes point up traditional features in a chart comes from one of the first charts run on the computer after the program was developed to make the geocentric positions for the planetary nodes available. This man had a wide Venus-Saturn conjunction that squared his Ascendant, thus ample evidence of a problem in the area of affections. When the nodes were added to the picture, the south node of Venus fell exactly on the Ascendant, and when progressed Venus reached his Descendant, he had an operation on his throat. Progressed Venus was in Taurus at the time, one of the two signs Venus is said to rule, and Taurus traditionally rules the throat.

Another striking case involved a girl who was born with defective female organs. Venus was square a Saturn-Neptune conjunction and also quincunx the Moon, the latter in the health house (sixth) conjunct both Pluto and South Moon. Again, we have ample evidence of difficulty in the area of love, with sexual implications since the Moon, the south node of the Moon, and Pluto were in Leo. But again, for further emphasis, especially indicative of the intense nature of the problem, both the nodes of Venus were conjunct the natal Sun and Midheaven.

Still another unusual case put the south node of Venus on a Venus-Uranus conjunction square Neptune in the fifth house (children) and also square the Moon in the eleventh house. The Moon also ruled Cancer on the cusp of the fifth. This woman deeply wanted a child but never had one, as is often the case with a negatively aspected Neptune in or ruling the fifth, but she had a tumor with hair and fingernails, which might be considered an attempt by the body to produce the desired infant. A blend of love and creative imagination (Venus, Neptune, and the Moon) can do remarkable things, but in this instance the result brought more headache than happiness.

In another example, a woman became ill when progressed Venus reached her south node of Venus, and the problem seemed to be largely psychosomatic, stemming from loneliness and hunger for a love relationship. In contrast, Henry Ford's south Venus conjunct natal Venus in Virgo in the tenth house of career and status and square his Uranus in the seventh house of close relationships and competition, seems to be an additional key to his climb to power and success with a mixture of service and penny-pinching in a highly competitive business. As is usual in the charts of highly prominent people, there were many exact nodal aspects in Ford's chart, including aspects from both nodes of Mercury, Mars, Neptune, and Pluto; and from the south nodes of Jupiter, Saturn, and Uranus in addition to South Venus already mentioned. Perhaps this array of power from all the south nodes is a clue to the urge to give, which lies behind the Ford Foundation and its grants for educational and research causes.

Some interesting variations on the handling of Venus matters can be seen in the charts of some political figures. Jerry Brown, governor of California and a chronic bachelor at age 41, has his North Venus conjunct his Uranus in Taurus in the tenth house. Natal Venus and Mercury are also in a wider conjunction to Uranus. John Kennedy, former president of the U.S., with South Venus conjunct natal Mars (and more widely Mercury and Jupiter, with all square Uranus, eighth house Taurus to fourth house Aquarius) was married but reported to have indulged in considerable extra-curricular playing. Rosalynn Carter, devoted wife of the current U.S. president, has North Venus conjunct her Juno in Cancer, and Juno is very widely conjunct natal Pluto. Former President Ford and his wife Betty have interesting aspects. Gerry Ford's Venus nodes form an exact yod (double quincunx) to his tenth house Uranus, repeating the message of other factors that his work constantly took him away from his family. Betty Ford has North Venus conjunct her Vesta, just inside the eighth house and her South Venus conjunct her natal Venus in the sixth house. Vesta and the sixth house both point to the choice of a partner highly committed to his work.

Mars

Aspects to the nodes of Mars offer predictable areas of stress, action, health concerns, self-assertion, urge to freedom, and sometimes violence, depending on context and degree of conflict. One interesting case is a woman who has been unable to relate to male peers. She does not have the Venus-Mars square that, traditionally, suggests friction with peers of the opposite sex, but she does have the south node of Venus square the north node of Mars and the south node of Mars square the north node of Venus. In a case of an anxiety neurosis, South Venus and South Uranus fell on a conjunction of Saturn and Sun. A wide conjunction of these with the south node of the Moon offered additional clues to self-doubt and tension and further evidence of the paralysis of action came from South Mars conjunct natal Mars with North Mars sesquisquare.

A man currently dying of cancer has South Mars conjunct natal Mars in Scorpio, exactly square Saturn in Leo, reinforcing the danger of self-blocking, which can lead to illness when the energy is turned in against the self. The case of the child with the defective brain has been mentioned, but since Mars traditionally rules the brain, it is appropriate to mention again that South Mars in the chart was conjunct Neptune in the tenth house. Neptune often points to problems with mysterious, little understood causes, and the tenth house relates to law on all levels and the consequences of past action.

In contrast, a teenage boy turned his self-will outward, and ran from home repeatedly, finally ending in the hands of juvenile authorities. He had South Mercury opposite natal Mars, North Uranus square natal Moon, North Mars square Mercury, and South Mars square the Part of Fortune. The need to rebel and to strike out for freedom is obvious in these patterns.

Patricia Hearst became a rebel temporarily, joining with her SLA captors. She has North Mars square natal Uranus and sesquisquare the natal Ascendant, and south Mars semisquare natal Saturn. One of my most tragic cases involves a sixteen-year-old boy who killed three young girls aged eight to ten, the same age as his sister. Among other node aspects, progressed South Mars was one minute of arc from the exact square to natal Ascendant.

In the chart of a baby who was kidnapped when only a few weeks old and never found, the square of South Mars to the nodes of the Moon is only a fragment of the picture that included stress aspects from both nodes of Mercury and Venus in addition to stress aspects from the south nodes of Jupiter, Saturn, Uranus, and Neptune. Among the aspects were several separating quincunxes and oppositions, including the yod (double quincunx) of South Uranus to Saturn and Venus. Remember that these node aspects are exact to one-degree orb as are all examples given in this volume.

Two more striking cases come from the Kennedy family. John Kennedy had South Mars on his natal Ascendant while Robert Kennedy had South Mars quincunx his Washington Ascendant and North Mars conjunct his Los Angeles Ascendant, the latter being the place where he was assassinated. To complete the picture, Robert's natal Mars exactly opposed his natal Ascendant.

Continuing with political figures, we can note that former president of the U.S. Richard Nixon has North Mars conjunct his North Moon in Aries in the seventh house, lending a bit more support to his paranoia. Former Secretary of State Henry Kissinger, who was noted for his "single-handed" diplomacy, sometimes jokingly referred to as "the Lone Ranger," has North Mars conjunct his Antivertex, which functions as an auxiliary Ascendant, and South Mars conjunct his natal Moon in Libra. The latter offered a clue to his broken marriage. Madalyn O'Hara, who carried a legal fight to the Supreme Court and succeeded in barring the reciting of prayers in public schools, has South Mars on her natal Descendant, a clue to power struggles, whether with a mate, or with the public.

But Mars can also be a sense of personal uniqueness, and the courage to pioneer. Two of the most original of our modern psychotherapists are Jean Houston, who has the nodes of Mars conjunct and opposite her natal Sun in the ninth house, with Uranus in a slightly wider conjunction with the Sun; and R.D. Laing who has North Mars on his IC and South Mars on his seventh house Mercury in Scorpio. As you might imagine, his ideas are highly controversial!

Jupiter
Despite its reputation as the great benefactor, Jupiter can also be a clue to excesses and consequent problems, and its nodes are apparently similar, bringing faith and intelligence and good judgment when manifested harmoniously, or the reverse when expressed as poor judgment. Whether or not the traditional luck associated with Jupiter is really an unearned bonus or the consequence of constructive attitudes and understanding, Jupiter's nodes appear to be a key to faith and to the fortune that comes from confidence. For example, Aimee Semple McPherson, the founder of a modern church, had aspects from both nodes of Jupiter in her chart, North Jupiter to her Midheaven. and South Jupiter to Mer-

cury, while the north node of Mars aspected natal Jupiter. Another minister, though not a famous one, has south Jupiter aspecting natal Jupiter. The daughter of a minister, who says that her father's work was the single most influential factor in her early life, has North Jupiter conjunct her IC.

The philosopher-astrologer, Dane Rudhyar, has North Jupiter conjunct natal Jupiter while South Mars opposes them, adding energy to the search for meaning in life and the prolific writing and publication. Natal Venus is sextile/trine the node-Jupiter opposition, helping to harmonize and add the capacity for artistic expression. North Uranus conjunct Mars adds additional drive to the search for new knowledge and especially to the interest in astrology associated with Uranus. The missionary zeal of Mars-Jupiter aspects appears strongly in Timothy Leary, proponent of psychedelic sacraments. His chart includes north Venus conjunct Jupiter, south Mars sextile Jupiter, north Jupiter sextile Saturn, south Jupiter sextile Uranus, south Uranus square Jupiter, and north Neptune conjunct Neptune. Other contacts which are less directly associated with philosophical, mystical interests include north Saturn square Sun and north Mars quincunx Mars, and the large number of planetary-node exact aspects are a typical key to prominence and impact on society. Mir Bashi took an unusual counseling path, becoming a highly successful and internationally known palmist. Bashi had his progressed Jupiter on North Venus and North Neptune for years while North Jupiter is on North Moon—all conducive to success.

But Jupiter aspects, even "good" ones, are no guarantee against problems in the life. In fact, Jupiter often figures prominently in the release of someone to the next level of life or anticipations of such release as an escape from problems. For example, one woman with North Venus square natal Jupiter and North Jupiter conjunct natal Pluto planned to commit suicide, but stopped before carrying it through. Another individual, a highly educated man with Jupiter in good aspect to the nodes of the Moon, actually carried it through. The violence that he eventually turned against himself was suggested by aspects of Mars' nodes to Uranus and Jupiter along with a depressive conjunction of South Saturn on Mercury in Capricorn in the twelfth house. In a case of the accidental death of an eight-year-old boy, North Jupiter opposed natal Jupiter in the fourth house while South Jupiter was quincunx natal Uranus in the twelfth, again the classical aspects of separation, the opposition and quincunx, to the water houses that mark the end of the cycle. In still another chart of accidental death, North Jupiter opposed Pluto in the twelfth house. Perhaps the warning against taking fragments out of context should be repeated at this time, since in all these cases the balance of the aspects clearly showed the crisis of the situation, and the Jupiter aspects may suggest the release to a higher level of existence. Jupiter can symbolize the basic faith that things will be better somewhere else; if this world has become unbearable, let's try another one.

The range of possible manifestations of the same basic principle can also be illustrated by the charts of two vastly different individuals who still shared a commitment to the search for final truth—Carl Jung, the famous Swiss psychotherapist and writer, and Muhammad Ali, famous boxer who converted to Islam, and took on the U.S. government in a battle for his beliefs. Jung had North Jupiter conjunct his natal sixth house Mercury, supporting his intellectual focus, a life devoted to research, writing, and counseling. Ali has North Vesta and North Jupiter conjunct each other and the Antivertex, fitting his identification (Antivertex) with work (Vesta) and with a personally chosen religious faith (Jupiter). A high value placed on work and the probability of success is another way to interpret the combination.

Listing an individual under one node rather than another is always somewhat arbitrary, since there are normally multiple contacts, confirming the same basic themes. This "syndrome" situation is also present in tabulations of groups of charts. For example, we have the totals for aspects of planetary nodes to planets for a small group of thirty-one religious celibates (priests and nuns in Roman Catholic orders) and for ninety-five individuals (both male and female) in a relatively small recent religious sect in the U.S. The numbers are too small to be statistically significant, but there are suggestive emphases in both groups. In the Catholic group, the north nodes are more evenly distributed, with more aspects from nodes to Venus Vesta, and Mars. The south nodes show clearer patterns, with the largest numbers of aspects formed by South Saturn and South Pluto, fitting the self-discipline, self-mastery, austerity, or Puritan virtue idea. Individual patterns include a higher number of aspects of South Jupiter to Vesta and South Vesta to Jupiter as well as South Pluto to Vesta. There are also a larger number of South Saturn aspects to Jupiter and of South Mars to Saturn, all fitting the principle of self-restraint in a religious vocation. Obviously, one could not predict such an outcome. We can only say that the results fit the basic principles.

In the small, new religious sect, North Pallas, North Uranus, and North Jupiter have the largest total number of aspects to the planets and chart angles. On the other hand, Vesta and Pluto are the planets having the largest number of aspects from the combined north nodes of the planets. In the node totals, South Mars has the most aspects, with Pallas, Ceres, Venus, Vesta, and Uranus next in order, not far behind. Saturn and Jupiter are the planets with the most aspects to south nodes. Again, the emphasis makes psychological sense for a group that emphasized community living (Pallas) rather than marriage (Juno), and a transpersonal emphasis (Jupiter, Saturn, Uranus) with Vesta for commitment and celibacy on the part of the leaders. The emphasis on South Mars may reflect the group limitation on individual freedom. The sect felt separated from the general society but insisted on total conformity by the members to the revelations of the founder.

Saturn
The geocentric nodes of Saturn, like the preceding ones, appear to follow the patterns associated with the planet from which they are derived. They may mark areas of severe restriction and limits as already described for the baby born virtually without a brain who had south Saturn and south Pluto exactly on the natal Ascen-

dant. Or they may mark the danger of overreaching and a fall. This occurred figuratively in the case of Robert Kennedy, who had the same two points—South Saturn and South Pluto—on his Midheaven, showing his drive for power and the odds against reaching it. It occurred literally in the case of a woman who fell to her death with North Saturn on Pluto in the twelfth house, South Saturn opposite Mars in the twelfth house, as well as South Pluto conjunct a natal Saturn-Moon conjunction in the sixth house of health. With the Sun the natural ruler of the sign of children, a woman who died in childbirth had North Saturn conjunct and South Saturn opposite her natal Sun. South Saturn opposed the tenth house natal Saturn of President Kennedy, while his north Saturn squared his Ascendant.

A remarkably high percentage of individuals who reach positions of political power seem to have close aspects to the nodes of Saturn and/or Pluto. To list a few who have recently been president or vice president of the U.S., or have run for these positions, our current president, Jimmy Carter, has North Saturn on his natal Midheaven. Vice President Mondale has North Saturn opposite his Vesta and South Saturn conjunct his Ceres. These are the two asteroids associated with Virgo (work). The nodes of Vesta, the real Virgo workaholic, fall conjunct and opposite Mondale's Sun. For further drive, North Mars is on his Washington Ascendant. Former President Ford has the Saturn nodes almost opposite each other, falling across the midpoint of Sun/IC. North Saturn moved by progression to the exact conjunction with the IC. while Ford was still a baby. It remained in that aspect, or conjunct his Sun, until he was well into maturity, by which time North Pluto had moved in to conjunct his natal Sun, a position that is still exact within one degree. Ford has also had progressed Jupiter in Capricorn conjunct South Vesta for a good many years of his life, further testimony to his career drive.

Former Vice President Rockefeller had many node contacts, including North Jupiter conjunct Mercury; South Vesta opposite Venus and conjunct Uranus (a key to the broken marriage); North

Vesta conjunct Neptune; North Saturn conjunct the Midheaven and progressed south Saturn stayed opposite his Midheaven for years. He also had progressed Saturn opposite North Mars for years; both the last two aspects suggesting his inability to achieve the power he wanted so much—the presidency. For former President Nixon, progressed Neptune stayed conjunct North Saturn most of his life, as well as conjunct his Washington Midheaven. South Saturn progressed to oppose his Neptune and was opposite the Washington Midheaven. Nixon also had the nodes of Pluto conjunct and opposite his Sun and square his Washington Ascendant. North Jupiter squared his Moon's nodes and South Uranus opposed his natal Midheaven among other node aspects. Thomas Eagleton who made an unsuccessful bid for the vice presidency and was dumped by McGovern when his mental history came out, has North Saturn square his Midheaven while south Saturn is square his Pluto and quincunx his Washington Ascendant. South Pluto is also opposite natal Pluto. Hubert Humphrey, who also tried for the presidency, had progressed Uranus opposite his South Saturn for most of his life in addition to North Pluto conjunct his Neptune. Ronald Reagan, who still seems to have his eye on the presidency, has both North Saturn and North Pluto on his first house Neptune, while South Saturn is opposite his Washington Ascendant if his birth time is accurate. Enough is enough, but just coincidentally, Jerry Brown, who is somewhat impatiently waiting in the wings, has South Saturn opposite his Pluto (at the midpoint of Moon-Ascendant), while North Saturn squares his Aries Sun. Although most of my charts of "power people" are from the U.S., we can note that the recent prime minister of India, M. Desai, has South Saturn conjunct his Mars. North Saturn and South Jupiter are square his Venus but sextile-trine his Moon, and there are many other node aspects.

Executive power (the Saturn principle) can be used well or badly. As a final footnote to this impressive run-down, I have the chart of Jim Jones, the man personally responsible for the deaths of over 800 people in the jungles of Guyana, plus charts of two of his leaders who died with him. Jones had a close Vesta-Saturn-East

Point conjunction in Capricorn in his first house opposite Jupiter and Pluto in Cancer in the seventh house, square Uranus and Venus in Aries in the third house (and other Aries factors more widely). The north and south nodes of Saturn, Pluto, and Vesta, natal and progressed, were all involved in the pattern, repeating the conflict theme with incredible emphasis. His woman follower, born the year before Jones, had some of the cardinal squares with the nodes of Jupiter, Saturn, and Pluto in aspect, and North Uranus on the IC. The male follower was born the year after Jones, also connected through cardinal squares and similar node aspects. Both were highly idealistic people apparently taken in by Jones. The woman had Pisces in the first house and Mars conjunct Jupiter, a frequent missionary combination. The personal savior theme was even stronger in the man, with a first house Neptune, Jupiter conjunct the Ascendant from the twelfth house, and loaded ninth and twelfth houses. His south node of the Moon was in an earth sign and house and Saturn in an earth house, showing his lesson was to become realistic. The woman follower also had Saturn in an earth sign, and her Guyana progressed Ascendant opposed it at the time of her death. Bringing ideals down into effective manifestation in the material world, integrating the spiritual and the physical, is the name of the game but no one said it was easy.

Uranus

We expect the unexpected, the innovative, the adventurous, the humanitarian or the crackpot revolutionary from Uranus, and the geocentric nodes are no exceptions. The boy who kept running away from home has already been mentioned with his strong aspects involving nodes of Uranus and Mars. Similar Mars-Uranus node aspects figured in the chart of the suicide. The woman who died in childbirth had North Uranus and North Mars conjunct natal Uranus in the eighth house (the end of a cycle), in addition to many stress aspects from planetary nodes. North Uranus squared the natal Sun in the boy who died accidently at age eight. Another runaway child, this one a girl who was eventually found murdered by an unknown assailant, had North Uranus square Mars in the first house and South Uranus square the natal Ascendant as part of the picture of a person unable to accept restriction. Many additional stress aspects to the nodes were present in the chart, including aspects to both nodes of Saturn, South Mercury, North Venus, South Mars, South Jupiter, South Neptune and North Pluto. At the risk of repetition, remember these node aspects are exact within a one-degree orb (unlike the usual wide orbs allowed for planetary aspects). It is the number and exactness of aspects that suggest the extreme qualities associated with such charts.

As another kind of rebel, Karl Marx, father of Communist doctrine, had South Uranus on his natal Midheaven (natal Uranus was only four degrees from it, farther into the tenth house) and the Uranus node squared Saturn in the first house—a classical picture of a revolt against authority, tradition, and power. Hitler had South Uranus in a yod (double quincunx) to his node of the Moon and his Mars-Venus conjunction, showing his separation from and problems with close relationships. Dean Corll, the Houston, Texas murderer of several teenage boys, had natal Moon and Mercury in opposition across Gemini-Sagittarius, in the tenth and fourth houses. North Uranus was opposite Mercury and South Uranus opposite Moon, both within eight minutes of arc, intensifying his rejection of any outside limits, which was shown in the chart by many planetary aspects. His planetary aspects included a Vesta-Saturn-South Moon conjunction in Aries in the ninth house square Pluto-Pallas in early Leo in the twelfth, Venus in late Capricorn in the sixth, and the Aries group was also quincunx Neptune in Virgo, which opposed the Mars in Pisces. The Mercury-Moon opposition was octile and trioctile the cardinal cross. Other node aspects included South Mercury square Ceres and quincunx Uranus; South Venus square Neptune; South Ceres square Mars; North Saturn square the Moon's nodes, and the nodes of Pluto on the Vertex axis.

A more pleasant form of Uranian expression finds its outlet through psychic openness. All professional psychics who were checked had aspects to one or both nodes of Uranus. For example,

Edgar Cayce had North Uranus in aspect to the nodes of the Moon and to Mars while South Uranus aspected Venus and the Midheaven. The birth date obtained from Arthur Ford, a different one than the published version, puts North Uranus conjunct a Mars-Pluto conjunction. The charts of other less well-known psychics included such aspects as North Uranus to natal Uranus and South Uranus to Ascendant for one; North Uranus to Pluto and again South Uranus to Ascendant for another; and North Uranus to Saturn for a third. Development of the capacity to share information that was obtained psychically may be especially related to aspects between Uranus nodes and the angles of the chart, or water planets. A female psychic has North Uranus conjunct her Moon. Famous psychic Uri Geller has North Uranus sextile his tenth house Pluto from the midpoint of his North Moon conjunct Vertex in the eighth house. North Uranus is also trioctile his Ascendant. Elizabeth Kubler-Ross, who has become very involved in the psychic scene, has north Uranus conjunct her IC and semisextile her Sun-Pluto conjunction.

Neptune

With the nodes of Neptune, we seem to find extremes of artistic or spiritual gifts on the one hand versus mysterious health problems and various forms of escapism, including the release to higher levels, on the other hand. Examples of artistic involvement include Joan Baez who has South Neptune trine Venus, and Donovan whose North Neptune is conjunct Pluto (which is in turn conjunct Mars) and South Venus opposite Neptune. A Hollywood singer and composer's North Neptune is conjunct his second-house Venus.

A minister with South Neptune opposite his Moon, and Aimee McPherson who had South Neptune aspecting Mars in the tenth house, are examples of spiritual concerns. Billy Graham, famous Baptist globe trotter, has South Neptune opposite natal Neptune in Leo, with progressed Neptune maintaining the aspect throughout his life. He also has North Uranus on his North Moon. Former Baptist minister, turned psychic, Paul Solomon has both North

Neptune and South Mercury conjunct his twelfth house Mercury in Leo. The new Catholic pope from Poland has north Neptune conjunct natal Neptune, and his natal Jupiter is just two degrees from his Neptune. Incidentally, our newest astrological tool, Chiron, which I suspect symbolizes its namesake, Sagittarius, is in 9 Aries in the Pope's chart, exactly trine his Neptune and its node.

An example of the health focus occurs in a baby born blind and mentally defective who has south Neptune conjunct her Moon in the sixth house of health, with the Moon involved in a whole network of stress aspects to other planets. South Neptune squared the Midheaven and IC in the child born without a brain, reinforcing the interpretation of circumstances brought from the past that are present from birth. North Neptune was conjunct the Midheaven and opposite the IC in the chart of the woman who died in childbirth.

We did not find any major emphasis on aspects from the nodes of Neptune to planets or from planetary nodes to Neptune in the charts of the religious celibates or the small, recent sect for which we have collections of data. But we did find the nodes of Neptune strong in the charts of 203 alcoholics for whom we have timed births. North Neptune had the highest number of aspects to the planets and angles in our sample, with North Uranus next highest. Among the south nodes, South Venus had the largest number of aspects, with Ceres, Pallas, and Neptune close behind. To add more weight to the pattern, the largest number of aspects from all planetary north nodes occurred with Mercury and Neptune. The south nodes of the planets, in contrast, singled out Venus, Mars, and Jupiter for the highest total number of aspects.

As in the balance of the cases cited, the context is necessary before even tentative conclusions can be offered as to how the patterns are likely to manifest.

Pluto
As Pluto is the last planet to be discovered and, therefore, with less accumulated data on its symbolic nature in a horoscope, it

nevertheless seems reasonably close to the nature of the sign most astrologers associate with it—Scorpio. The core meaning of letter eight in our astrological alphabet (Pluto and its nodes, Scorpio, eighth house, etc.) seems to be a search for self-knowledge and self-mastery, generally learned through interaction with others. The goal is to learn to give, receive, and share joint possessions and pleasures. But where the drive for mastery is turned out against others instead of inward to control the self, we may find a ruthless use of power. When the self-control is overdone, we may find extremes of self-blocking, up to the point of surgery and death. The search for self-awareness may lead one to depth psychology, involvement with occult things, and psychic ability.

Several examples in which the Pluto nodes were involved have already been mentioned in describing earlier planets. Not yet mentioned is the fact that the north nodes of both Saturn and Pluto were square Uranus in the twelfth house in the chart of Hitler. Already mentioned are the combination of the south nodes of both these planets on the Midheaven of Robert Kennedy and John Kennedy's nodes of Pluto square his Ascendant. The south nodes of both Saturn and Pluto opposed natal Pluto across the twelfth and sixth houses in the chart of the girl who attempted suicide but desisted in the middle of the act. A similar pattern of South Pluto opposite natal Pluto from the twelfth house to the sixth house occurred in the chart of a person who carried out the suicide, but his North Saturn opposed his Ascendant while his South Saturn was conjunct Mercury in Capricorn in the twelfth, as already noted. The whole pattern is potentially depressive and self-defeating. The nodes of Pluto and Saturn also figured prominently with natal Mars, Pluto, Saturn and the Moon, and again across the twelfth and sixth houses in the chart of the girl who fell to her death.

Two murderers who have already been mentioned include Dean Corll who had the nodes of Pluto on his Vertex axis, and the sixteen-year-old boy who killed three friends of his young sister. The latter had North Pluto conjunct his natal Ascendant with South Saturn opposite it. North Vesta and North Venus were opposite his seventh house Saturn in Capricorn, and progressed Saturn had maintained the exact aspect, while his progressed Midheaven had moved in to square the natal Ascendant, North Pluto, and South Saturn at the time of the murders.

The variety of possible manifestations of a single principle can be illustrated by Joan Baez and a female astrologer. Both have the nodes of Pluto conjunct and opposite their Sun. Baez used the power drive in healthy ways to reach success and fight for her beliefs in Viet Nam. Initially, she opposed the U.S. involvement there, but reproached the Viet Cong for their betrayal of human rights. The astrologer has also used the drive for personal success but is struggling for self-mastery over food and is overweight.

Among well-known individuals concerned in various ways with mind power and the search for or promotion of their own brand of "truth," we can list Ram Dass with North Pluto on his Ascendant, South Pallas and South Juno on his Midheaven, South Ceres opposite his Jupiter, North Ceres conjunct his Antivertex, and South Venus opposite his Pallas. Like Jerry Brown, he has neither married nor had children, but has devoted his life to the transpersonal area, working with humanity and social causes.

Jose Silva, the founder of Mind Control, has South Pluto square Moon, South Uranus opposite Vesta, North Neptune semisquare Ascendant, and South Jupiter opposite Pluto. Daddy Bray, Hawaiian Kahuna psychic and healer, had North Pluto conjunct North Moon. Werner Erhard has South Pluto and South Saturn conjunct North Moon, and North Jupiter conjunct South Moon. Riley Crabb, whose life work involves a journal on anything psychic, has South Pluto opposite Neptune and South Uranus conjunct Jupiter. Maharaj Ji, the teenage Hindu leader of a religious group, has North Pluto conjunct his tenth house Cancer Moon, South Saturn opposite the Moon, and North Jupiter conjunct his Midheaven

Aspects in the chart of an institutionalized, psychotic male include South Pluto opposite Venus and square Ascendant, South Neptune opposite Mercury, North Neptune opposite Moon, South

Mercury conjunct Mercury, North Vesta conjunct Uranus and South Jupiter square Pluto and Pallas, the latter two opposite each other. The planetary nodes accentuate a grand cross in fixed signs involving Jupiter, Mercury, Mars, and Moon, and the individual alternated between power struggles with the world and a retreat into his own imaginary world.

The section on Saturn mentioned many people involved with power who also have Pluto node aspects. Henry Ford surmounted the square of both Pluto nodes to his Jupiter, but Martin Luther King Jr. was assassinated with progressed Venus square both nodes of Pluto. South Pluto conjunct the Midheaven may be one key to the rise to prominence of a well-known California psychic, and Edgar Cayce's South Pluto aspected his natal Uranus in the twelfth house, a contact between two planets, which theoretically offer clues to the psychic talent. Again we are reminded that the context of the whole chart must be kept clearly in mind and the capacity of the individual to integrate and express harmoniously even those patterns which suggest conflict. In the end, it is only by the fruits of the life that we can judge the "age" of the soul.

The Asteroids: Ceres, Pallas, Juno, and Vesta

The asteroids are small planets, mostly orbiting the Sun in the area between Mars and Jupiter. The four included in this volume were originally discovered during the interval from 1800 to 1807, but they were first offered to U.S. astrologers in an ephemeris published in 1973. Some years later, TIA offered a more complete and more accurate ephemeris of their longitudes and declinations, and this edition of *The Node Book* presents their geocentric node positions. Obviously, conclusions must remain tentative in view of the short period during which they have been studied by astrologers, but even the fragmentary work completed to date seems to support the general theory that the nodes of the stellar body symbolize the same psychological principle as does the body itself. There will undoubtedly be controversy over meanings for a good many years and the suggested interpretations offered here are mainly based on the personal experience of the author Zipporah Dobyns.

Ceres and Vesta seem associated with the Virgo themes of work and efficient functioning in general. But Ceres has strong Cancer overtones, suggesting a kind of "Earth Mother" quality. I have been interpreting its position (sign, house, and aspects) as keys to the individual's experience of being mothered, and of mothering others, and the feedback is consistently positive. Any new tool in astrology is first tested in this way—by asking questions of the client to check both its meaning in the natal chart and the nature of events when the astrological factor is prominent by current aspect. Ceres seems to operate largely as a nurturing urge or desire to be nurtured in practical ways. When in heavy stress aspects, there are difficulties in achieving the desire due to conflicts with other psychological components of the individual.

Vesta seems to be the true Virgo "workaholic" with a potential for total immersion in the job to the exclusion of all else. This "all-or-none" tendency can result in outstanding success in the work, or in enormous frustration in people who have not found a job to which they can give this dedication, and such frustration is a common cause of illness. Illness gets us out of the job we hate. It is also common to find some sort of alienation or loss in personal relationships when Vesta is prominent. This may be by conscious choice if the subject has found fulfilling work, or it may be seen as something thrust upon the person by forces beyond personal control when the conflict is operating at a subconscious level. An obviously oversimplified rule of thumb but with an important kernel of truth is: if you want to know what your unconscious wants, look at what you have. The unconscious (almost) always wins in a conflict with the conscious drives, and it pays to stay in touch and try to work with the unconscious. Astrology is, of course, one of the most effective ways to spot such conscious-unconscious conflicts with water (planets, signs, houses) always suggesting some component of the unconscious.

To return to Vesta, a phenomenal number of charts of people who have given their life to their work, and have made major contributions to the world through their work, show the prominent

Vesta. A much more limited amount of attention has been given to the nodes of the asteroids, but the same trend is apparent. The nodes of Vesta seem to support the tendency to be "married" to one's work when they appear in close aspect to angles or planets. Ronald Reagan, with his eye still on the U.S. presidency at the age of sixty-eight, has North Vesta conjunct his Uranus in Capricorn. Indira Gandhi has her progressed Neptune on her North Vesta for a major part of her life, with her natal Saturn in a wider conjunction to her Neptune, both in Leo. A male whose mother died when he was a baby, and who was married to four women simultaneously in different countries (searching for the lost mother) had South Ceres opposite his natal Pluto in Cancer (Pluto and Saturn strad-dling the fourth house cusp), while progressed Pluto retrograded to conjunct North Vesta about the time the mother died.

Jean Houston, a leading psychotherapist who has chosen to give her life to work rather than to have children, has south Vesta conjunct her natal Moon in Aquarius in the fifth house. To repeat the theme, South Ceres in Capricorn in the fourth house squares her natal Vesta in Aries. R.D. Laing, a well-known English psy-chotherapist, has South Ceres conjunct natal Saturn and South Vesta conjunct natal Ceres. Fritz Perls, founder of Gestalt psycho-therapy, had progressed North Vesta conjunct his Vesta-Sun-Ceres tight conjunction in Cancer in the twelfth house for his first ten years of life, years which are considered highly important as "setting up" the basic life patterns. And his original mentor Sigmund Freud, from whom he later broke, had North Vesta con-junct his natal Saturn, reinforcing the emphasis on work.

Madalyn O'Hara, the militant atheist who fought a battle to the Supreme Court to prevent prayer in schools, has north Vesta con-junct her Ascendant. Obviously, many factors in her chart point to her stormy, "no quarter" life style, but the Vesta node seems to say it again, including the danger of considerable personal alienation with the south Mars opposition Ascendant already mentioned in the section on Mars. Still another person with outstanding career success but much alienation in her personal life was Joan

Crawford. Her birth time is variously given as 10:18 pm or 11:04 pm; it seems probably that she only knew it was late evening. A tentative rectification suggests that 9:05 pm might be a closer fit. But regardless of exact time, she had South Vesta conjunct her natal Moon-Saturn conjunction in Aquarius, to repeat the theme of her natal Vesta exactly conjunct natal Sun in Aries. Publications appearing since her death have described her destructive relationships with adopted children and a variety of men in her life. Among other node contacts, she also had South Mercury conjunct her Jupiter, South Mars trine her Venus with North Jupiter opposite South Mars and if my suspected birth time is accurate, the North Mars-South Jupiter opposition fell on her Vertex axis while North Venus was on her Descendant.

There are endless variations on the possible conflict between domesticity and a career outside the home. Jean Houston solved the conflict by not having children. Joan Crawford adopted them but was apparently unable to provide the nurturing warmth so important to young children. Her career always came first. Indira Gandhi offers still a third variation. She let her feelings for her children interfere with her career. She trusted and favored a son, Sanjay, who took advantage of his position and was, in part, responsible for her fall. A long-time resident in India says that he was the most hated man in the country, and he is currently under investigation for financial misconduct. The danger of idealizing family too much and having to learn a lesson in that area is said in Indira's chart repeatedly: Sagittarius on the fifth cusp and Capricorn in the fifth house; Neptune and Saturn conjunct in Leo; south node of the Moon in Cancer. The planetary nodes just say it again, with North Ceres conjunct South Moon; North Vesta conjunct progressed Neptune; and South Vesta conjunct progressed North Moon for most of her life.

Domesticity versus career (dependency versus dominance and achievement) is one of the dilemmas of life that can be identified as a challenge area in a horoscope. Some people solve the dilemma and manage to do a reasonably good job of both. Some choose to do one and project or repress the other, with consequent problems when the life drive, which has been relegated to the unconscious, comes out in uncomfortable ways. Some find sufficient satisfaction in one to give up the other without unconscious conflict. The crucial issue seems to be whether we are conscious of the conflict and able to resolve it on the conscious level. In the end, it is the results in the life that let us know how we are doing. Highly tentative conclusions to date suggest that a prominent Ceres, or its nodes, is helpful in resolving the dilemma of integrating career and family since Ceres seems able to combine the two naturally. A prominent Vesta, or its nodes, seems to compound the problem in light of its "all-or-none" tendency that can overemphasize one and lose perspective and proportion in relation to the other. But obviously the aspects are crucially important to indicate greater or lesser difficulty in integrating these differing drives in the nature. And, always, the context of the whole chart is essential. Anything important is said repeatedly.

Pallas and Juno, in contrast to the work theme associated with Ceres and Vesta, seem more concerned with personal relationships—a basic Libra focus. And as Ceres represents the "personal" side of Virgo and Vesta the "impersonal" side, Juno seems to be the "personal" side of Libran that wants marriage, and Pallas has many "impersonal" tendencies. I am still not clear on whether to associate Pallas with Sagittarius or with Aquarius overtones. It is often found prominent in consultants of all types, in people involved in social causes or concerned with knowledge, and in group activity of all sorts. Juno may well have Scorpio overtones, the other sign associated with close continuing relationships, where we learn to share really intense emotions, material possessions, and physical pleasures. Of course, sign and house placement can color this basic orientation. Pallas in signs or houses of personal relationships (Cancer, Leo, Libra, and Scorpio) will normally want home, marriage, and a family. Juno in the transpersonal signs or houses (Sagittarius through Pisces) may be involved in social causes. Both may be talented in the graphic arts. And Pallas, especially, may have some kind of perceptual problem such as difficulty in seeing patterns if found with conflict aspects, may have some kind of perceptual problem such as difficulty in seeing patterns.

Their nodes have been observed for too short a time to do more than suggest that they repeat the same themes as the planetary bodies. For example, the militant fighter to save the children of the world from orthodox religion, Madalyn O'Hara, has both South Pallas and South Juno in zero Aries exactly conjunct her eleventh house cusp. As the intersection of two great circles, the ecliptic and the equator, and the start of the seasonal zodiac, zero Aries is a highly important sensitive point in all charts. Aspects to it seem to tie the individual to the world scene. The eleventh house symbolizes the urge to go beyond convention and tradition, and as the fifth from the seventh house, it also symbolizes the children of others. The combination is highly appropriate for Madalyn O'Hara's impact on children. That the benefit of the impact is questionable, that she has a lesson in the area of nurturing children, might be suggested by her North Ceres conjunct South Moon in the twelfth house.

A few other examples of the Pallas attraction to careers in politics, as counselors, or just to changing the state of society in some way might include Francis Farrelly, a remarkable psychic diagnostician and healer, who has North Pallas conjunct her Virgo Sun while Albert Einstein had South Pallas conjunct his Pisces Sun. Ronald Reagan has South Pallas conjunct his natal Venus, fitting both the early career as a dancer and movie star and the later absorption in politics. The nodal axes of these two asteroids are very close, a further clue to their association with the urge for some kind of togetherness. In general, their nodes remain within a few degrees of each other. Their most frequent sign positions are Virgo for the north node and Pisces for the south node, a possible commentary on the human tendency to look for ideal relationships or to overrate their importance at times. As with any opposition, the goal is integration; in this case, of the ideal and the practical steps needed to reach it.

Among the examples where the nodes of both Pallas and Juno are featured together, we can list Jean Houston, the prominent psychotherapist who works with her husband in research and writing. She has a conjunction of South Pallas and natal Vesta in her seventh house, with South Venus and South Juno just past them on the eighth house cusp. Vesta brings the work theme, in Aries for pioneering areas and types of effort, with the eighth house, suggesting the shared research and royalties. For contrast, a young hyperactive child who has learning disabilities has both South Pallas and South Juno conjunct her ninth house Mercury, which is closely square her Ascendant. Uranus and Pluto are also conjunct Mercury and Vesta is opposite them, with the Ascendant being square the whole group.

Rosalynn Carter might be taken as an example of a devoted wife, and her North Pallas is on her first house Mars while her North Juno is on her local Ascendant in Washington D.C. Another devoted wife in my personal files has South Juno just a few minutes out of the one-degree orb to her natal Ascendant. In view of her "even-hour" birth time, I suspect that more precise timing would make the aspect exact. The man who married four women in four different countries had North Juno on his Vertex, which I read as an auxiliary seventh cusp symbolizing capacity to relate to others.

In the end, we cannot be reminded too often that the context of the chart is basic; the repeated theme is central in the nature. Many students wince at the thought of more complexity stemming from added factors. Once the metaphor of an alphabet is recognized, however, they see that having the same message repeated in capital letters, in italics, in lower case, etc. can only be helpful in getting the message. Think of the planetary nodes as another form of the twelve-letter alphabet of astrology, see if they repeat the themes shown in other ways in the horoscope, and then decide whether this new tool is helpful enough to be worth the effort of adding more symbols to an already crowded diagram. You may decide to consider them only in the charts of people who are especially important in your life. You may only want to add them in special cases such as twins where their aspects to angles can mark differences with a change of a few minutes in the birth time. A great many techniques and tools, ancient and modern, will be tested during the balance of this century, and I hope they pave the way to a truly helpful astrology of the twenty-first century.

Chapter 4

Nodes of the Moon

THE IMPORTANCE of the nodes of the Moon was recognized early in the development of astrology. The node cycles are basic in the computation of eclipses, which were awe inspiring events to early civilizations. A variety of nodal traditions are available for testing, including the theory that the placement of all the planets of the ancients (that is all except the outer three planets more recently discovered) on either side of the hemispheres formed by the nodal axis indicates a confined or sheltered life. The situation was said to end and the individual to move out of the enclosed state when one of the progressed planets crossed a node and thus moved into the opposite hemisphere.

The movement of the nodes is retrograde. Retrograde planets appear to be particularly inward in their action, an inward turning that may delay the full outer expression of the tendencies symbolized, or which may give it a stamp of unique individuality. The same inwardness or delay may also characterize the lunar node positions, as the individual experiences ambivalence over the contrasting drives of the opposing areas of life. Opposing signs and houses are natural partners. Each provides qualities needed by the other to make an effective team, but accomplishing the integration of these opposing qualities is often a basic challenge or developmental goal. Where integration is not achieved, the individual may swing like a pendulum from one side of the nodal axis to the other, first focusing on one, then on the other. Or the individual may concentrate on one side of the axis and avoid, repress, or project the other, with subsequent frustration. In projection, we find someone else to manifest that unaccepted part of ourselves, and the more we deny it in ourselves, the more the other person tends to do it to excess. It is quite possible to project good qualities, including potential talents. Or the nodal points may mark the scene of constant, never-ceasing activity, especially when they fall in mental signs and houses. Or a quality of intermittency may prevail, an on-again, off-again, stop-go state. Since the nodes are always actively engaged in their opposition to each other, they function as a continuing progressed aspect and maintain some degree of constant tension in the signs and houses in which they occur, so that change or action in the area is always possible.

As already indicated, it is imperative to always consider both house and sign position. Of course, aspects add power and importance to the indications as well as qualifications on action potential. For example, placement of the nodes in either Aries or Libra, or in the first and seventh houses, is associated with marital strain and difficulty in maintaining a permanent relationship in this area. It also appears frequently in the charts of counselors, consultants, and therapists, including Freud and Jung. These individuals may have considerable difficulty in their personal relationships but the ability to be intensely involved in a close relationship and yet to be able to release it in time is a positive and necessary capacity for a good therapist. If a counselor is unable to release clients, we may well have the interminable therapy characteristic of some of the older schools. Remember that there will always be a blend of sign and house, and adding a fixed sign or house to the mixture will tend toward greater stability and less flux, but at the same time the needed integration of the opposites may be rendered even more difficult to achieve. The result may be a kind of stalemate that periodically breaks loose explosively and then returns to the "same old stand." Fixed factors change, but only on their own terms.

As with the planetary nodes, the lunar nodes seem to carry some of the quality of the body from whose orbit they are derived.

The nodes of the Moon, like the Moon itself, seem to be associated with sensitivity and deep feeling, with a kind of emotional vulnerability that may be acutely uncomfortable when in stress aspects to such planets as Mars and Saturn. Often, if not most of the time, the lessons associated with the nodes come through close relationships. The Moon signifies our dependency needs and its nodes mark areas in which these needs are expressed and then are either fulfilled or blocked. Natal, progressed, and transiting positions all seem significant, and some of the most cohesive associations between two individuals are signaled by conjunctions of planets or angles in one person's chart with the lunar nodes of the other. Conjunctions with the south node of the Moon seem more pressured, but the tension of the opposition can also bring challenges and separation in the case of a north node conjunction. As with every factor in a chart, it is important to keep the nodes in the context of the whole chart, but they are a vital part of the whole. They do add clues to character and personality tendencies that might otherwise be missed or given less weight.

Unlike the examples given for the planetary nodes in which only exact aspects are used, examples given here for the nodes of the Moon include more traditional, wide orbs such as are used in computing planetary aspects. Research is needed in all areas of astrology, to validate the useful traditions and weed out the nonfunctional ones, but it is especially needed in this area of permissible orb for aspects. Cases listed are all from the mean nodes. The true nodes are too recent for comment at this time.

Aries-Libra or First House-Seventh House
The polar principles here are self-will and personal freedom as against limitations accepted in order to have relationships with others. The relationships of Libra and the seventh house may be cooperative or competitive, but if the sign or house is strongly occupied or aspected, the individual will seek peer associations as an important part of the life. Placing the nodes in either of these signs or these houses indicates the need to resolve the self-other tension. In the process, the individual may change marital or business part-

ners repeatedly or may stay in a state of tension in such relationships without actually breaking them. The position is also found often in the charts of high-powered business people such as Henry Ford. It also appears in the charts of politicians, a field associated with the Libra capacity for working toward a compromise solution. Richard Nixon has South Moon in Libra in the first house and North Moon in Aries in the seventh. Charles Dederich, founder of Synanon and noted for his work with drug addicts as well as alcoholics but also with a record of broken marriages, has the South Moon in Libra and the North in Aries. The woman mentioned as having fallen to her death had three broken marriages before the age of thirty with South Moon in Libra and North Moon in Aries.

Whether or not the self-other tension is a psychosomatic root of physical or psychological problems, a good many cases appear in which the south node in the first house or sign seems to indicate a problem in this area. For example, the baby born with a defective brain has South Moon in the first house. The connotation of some sort of threat to the person also appears in the chart of the kidnapped baby who also has South Moon in the first house. Edgar Cayce, who had South Moon in Virgo in the first house, could be characterized as a counselor or consultant from the house positions and as a healer from the sign positions. He also demonstrated another characteristic of the first house south Moon, which is the tendency to push the self too hard, a tendency that may stem partly from self-doubts and the need to find reassurance. Often, South Moon seems to function in a similar way to Saturn, indicating areas of self-doubt and anxiety and feelings of stress. The chart of a former nun has the lunar nodes in the same house position as Cayce, but in reverse signs. She had a long and successful career in her religious order, during which the tendencies of the nodes—delay and separation—in the area of partnership remained an accurate key to her state. She is now, at age fifty, considering marriage for the first time.

As should be apparent by now, the nodes must always be taken in context with the rest of the chart. Even in these few examples, we have listed individuals with no marriage, repeated marriages, and happy marriages who were involved in competitive business, politics, counseling, etc., people with critical or chronic physical or emotional challenges or with a sense of mission that leads them to dedicate their lives to humanity. With the South Node in the first house or in Aries, the problems are more likely to be personal. In Libra or the seventh house, the major strain comes through the relationship with others, but always they work as a team, either pulling against each other or, if integrated successfully, pulling together for the common cause. Though pressure and effort is almost certain to be associated with the south node, it is important not to assume crisis or failure. Often, just the sign and house position of the south node, even without considering aspects, will identify a key lesson area of the chart. For example, in a case of twins, one major difference between the two girls was that for the first, the south node fell in the seventh house, while for the later twin it had moved over the Descendant into the sixth house. Both girls were attractive and intelligent, yet their lives were strikingly different. The first had not married and was haunted by a pervasive anxiety in this area; the second was happily married and had a child but had hypochondriac tendencies that kept her running to the doctor for any small emotional upset.

Taurus-Scorpio or Second House-Eighth House

With this polarity we need to resolve the tension between, on the one hand, the natural self-indulgence and pleasure from owning and manipulating personal possessions, responding to or creating beauty in the world and, on the other side, the sense of obligation to learn to control our own appetites and to learn to respect the rights, possessions, and pleasures of others. The nodes in these positions may indicate a perpetual battle in the area of finances and possessions or sensuality between partners, whether or not legalized as such. Or the tension may operate internally in a battle of the appetites—alternately overeating and dieting, smoking and giving it up, drinking and trying to abstain, spending or giving and saving, and so forth. Where other people are involved, either one of the partners may be frustrated by the other's tendency to withhold or to be too free. For example, a woman with strong Leo in her chart married to a Capricorn who is primarily involved in his work, lives in a state of frustration over his lack of interest in sex. Her south node is in the eighth house. A man with both Taurus and Virgo strong in his chart battles between his urges toward natural sensuality (Taurus) and his urges toward celibacy and self-control (Virgo); his south node also falls in the eighth house. Another man with south node in Sagittarius in the eighth is so enraged at his wife's extravagance that he is unable to give his attention to achieving the wealth he desires until he has divorced her.

Sometimes the basic lesson is to learn to respect the rights and possessions of others. For example, two charts of individuals who steal compulsively (both under psychiatric care) have the south node in the eighth house. A very different example of a man, who might be described as almost obsessed with economic factors, property, and their relationship to power, is Karl Marx with his South Moon in the Scorpio sign and house. Sometimes this position seems to indicate a special challenge connected with death. The suicide mentioned in the chapter on planetary nodes, and also Martin Luther King, have the south node in Scorpio. As is obvious by now, the more critical position is in Scorpio or the eighth house, and the key lesson seems to be to learn insight, self-control, and the limits of self-will. But the Taurus-second house side has its problems, too. There may be heavy overindulgence on the one hand, or an inability to earn one's own way in the world, with a consequent tendency to look to others for support. But, just as the integrated Aries-Libra polarity shows the fine therapist or counselor, the integrated Taurus-Scorpio polarity shows someone with the capacity to enjoy the physical world and often to create much beauty and yet to also maintain a reasonable control over the appetites and to relate effectively with others in the area of sensuality. Often the north node in the eighth house suggests an individual to whom resources come easily, whether in the form of partner's income, inheritance, joint funds, or government grants. This is an excellent placement for research as well, with the urge to dig deep being characteristic of the water element while the earth side of the polarity wants to produce something in lasting, tangible form. In the end, as always, aspects from other features in the chart may give the major clue to the probable success of the effort to integrate, with sextile-trine aspects to the nodes suggesting success and the square aspects compounding the problems. But again, the context of the whole chart is a necessary part of any judgment, and fruits of the life tell the final story.

Gemini-Sagittarius or Third House-Ninth House
The challenge and potential here centers on mental capacity and the area of faith, *values,* and goals. The constant polar tension of the Moon's nodes across these signs and/or houses indicates constant mental activity, the potential for much travel (unless blocked by problems), and sometimes major *involvement* with relatives in the life. The strong urge to gain knowledge and then to give it to others makes this a frequent position in the chart of teachers of all varieties. In fact, it can turn up in the chart of anyone whose life centers around some field of communication. When negatively aspected to planets, angles, etc., problems that range from serious mental impairment (e.g., a female born blind and mentally challenged) to chronic anxiety or dissatisfaction from unrealized goals are likely. The problems are more common where South Moon is in Sagittarius or in the ninth house.

Examples of the latter placement occur in the case already mentioned of the anxiety neurosis that included South Moon in a wide conjunction with Saturn and Sun in Sagittarius in the third house. As it happens, Saturn and the South Moon fall within a degree of the 7 ½ degree aspect that is used in both the U.S. and Germany in predicting ionospheric disturbances. John Nelson of the U.S. and Dr. Theodor Landscheidt of West Germany use all multiples of 7½ degrees in their predictive work, and both claim accuracy of 90 percent or better.

A blend of unreasonable expectations and lack of faith appear in a case with South Moon in Sagittarius falling on the cusp of the eighth house but retrograding into the seventh house square Neptune in the fifth house. Saturn is again within a degree of the 7 ½ degree harmonic from South Moon in the eighth house. This girl's father committed suicide when she was barely into her teens, and she has continued to look for an impossible ideal in her love relationships (Neptune in the fifth) while at the same time she is afraid of losing her love as she lost her father and therefore holds back and cannot commit herself fully in a partnership (South Moon in the seventh). This is a good example of the challenge often found with South Moon in Sagittarius or in the ninth house in which the individual both hopes for too much and yet has either too little faith or a misplaced faith and therefore continues a vain search for inner peace.

Another case in which South Moon falls in Sagittarius puts it within a few minutes of the natal Moon in the twelfth house with Uranus more widely conjunct North Moon in the health house (sixth). This individual has a history of convulsive episodes and brief periods of amnesia. Additional aspects include Mercury in the ninth house in a square plus the 7½ degree harmonic to Uranus in the sixth, and Mercury in a closer but not exact square to the Ascendant. Still other examples include the already mentioned individual who attempted suicide who stopped voluntarily, as well as a successful suicide. Both had South Moon in Sagittarius, one in the tenth house and one in the twelfth. These houses, with their connotations of confrontation with forces partially outside the control of the individual (the law of the universe, including the consequences of past actions, and our own rooted subconscious habit patterns and emotional reactions) often mark areas of anxiety and stress.

A less drastic case of the nodes of the Moon in Gemini-Sagittarius puts them in the fifth and eleventh houses where they accentuate a drive for freedom and self-will and resistance to external discipline in the chart of the teenage runaway. Where the Gemini-Sagittarius positions of the nodes do not mark a problem in the area of self-confidence, especially about mental capacity, or problems in the area of faith, they often indicate tension with or obligations to relatives. This may range from sibling rivalry and competition, often over parental affection, to situations in which the individual is apparently able to learn needed lessons vicariously through the experience of relatives. In one example, the Moon's nodes fell in Taurus-Scorpio but in the third and ninth houses. The person involved successfully integrated them and developed a secure faith and then was able to help a sister whose daughter committed suicide and whose son died as the result of an accident. The individual herself did show one consequence typical of the nodes in these houses; she never finished her formal higher education, but she continued learning through personal readings and study. Often these nodal positions show constant changes in the area of study; changes of major field of study, of college, or the intermittent quality of periodically going back to school for more training. On the whole, unless very negatively aspected, these positions of the nodes seem to be readily integrated by a continuing concern with the world of the mind, learning, teaching, writing, traveling, etc.

Cancer-Capricorn or Fourth House-Tenth House

The characteristic tension of this nodal position seems primarily centered around a power struggle on some level. The motivating dynamics may be personal security or the desire to provide for the well-being of others, up to and including the homeland or humanity on occasion. It is a position found repeatedly in the charts of individuals in politics or playing a power role in life heading up their own business. Thus the Moon's nodes fall in these signs in the charts of Hitler, three Kennedys (Joseph, John, and Robert), former President Lyndon Johnson, the successful palmist Mir Bashir and Aimee Semple McPherson, who was one of the few women to successfully establish a church. The tenth house placement is common in the charts of individuals running their own business or profession, with North Moon in the tenth apparently bringing power and success more easily, but showing problems to be solved at home and often a neglect of home for the status drive; South Moon in the tenth more often showing someone who resists control by others, challenges the establishment and convention in some way, and may have secure roots in the family.

Often this placement of nodes in houses four and ten indicates tension in the early home between the parents. A broken home is frequent if there are strong squares to the nodes, either from death or divorce, with death somewhat more likely if water-earth signs are involved and divorce more likely with air-fire. On other occasions, it may indicate many changes of occupation of the father, or one who travels. Later, the individual may do the same, or there may be residence changes.

The principles to be integrated stem from the basic polarity of dependency-dominance; on the one hand, the need for emotional closeness and protection by a sheltering home and family is needed. On the other hand, the drive for power, which may also be motivated by security needs or by a sense of responsibility and obligation to make things work out according to accepted principles. When both signs (Cancer and Capricorn) or both houses (fourth and tenth) are occupied, as they are if the lunar nodes are there, the dependency need may be outweighed by the power need and the individual is likely to take the "mothering" role rather than that of the baby. This rejection of dependency can lead to the "Atlas" syndrome, with the world on the back and a need to remember that all life is interdependent.

When Cancer or the fourth house or the Moon are very strong, especially if supported by a strong Neptune and a focus in Pisces or in the twelfth house, the individual may use dependency as a means of control, such as physical or emotional illness or other forms of helplessness. Naturally, this is not usually a conscious action. Often, in fact, this position of the nodes, when heavily aspected, is a key to hereditary problems that may be present from birth and difficult to resolve. The basic insecurity can be a heavy burden, especially if not mitigated by a mixture of air-fire from other points in the chart, or if compounded by heavy aspects involving Saturn, Neptune and/or the Moon (the planets most prone to anxiety). Integration seems best achieved by gaining confidence through successful work in the world and by using the power attained to assist others. For many parents, the challenge is primarily experienced as time pressure as they try to do justice to both home-making and a career.

Leo-Aquarius or Fifth House-Eleventh House
The polar tension here may appear in the area of romance and friendship in which case the separating action of the nodes tends to delay a permanent love relationship and procreation. The fifth house rulership of children and the Aquarian urge to gain and give knowledge also makes this a typical position in the charts of teachers. Often, of course, both forms of action will be part of the picture, since many teachers marry late, and some spend their lives working with children without having their own. The reasons for the delay or avoidance of a permanent love-relationship may vary according to sign-house mixture from a search for perfection suggested by Sagittarius and/or Pisces, or to a fear of being dominated with Scorpio or Capricorn. The other side of the coin is a fear of losing freedom if Aries, Sagittarius, or Aquarius is involved. The extremes that can be found with this position of the lunar nodes range from teachers dedicated to the wellbeing of their students and to the gift of knowledge and implementation of humanitarian principles to serious problems in the area of sex, courtship, and children. For instance, the south node appears in the fifth house in the charts of some parents of illegitimate children, individuals unable to have children, or those with children having critical problems.

As an example of the last, the mother of the runaway girl who was later found murdered had previously lost a year-old baby. The mother had her South Moon in the fifth house. The runaway child also had her nodes in these houses, but in the signs of Cancer and Capricorn, and her life was one long struggle against submission to any will except her own until she met a force greater than her own. Ironic as it seems, this Leo-Aquarius position can as easily point to a school dropout as to a teacher, depending on aspects and of course the context of the whole chart. If the chart is one with a strong power drive or a need for individual freedom, there may be a drive for knowledge, but on the individual's own terms. If fire dominates the chart, the central motivating dynamic may be excitement and pleasure. That the drive was primarily for self-will in the runaway described above could be deduced from the fact that Uranus was widely conjunct her South Moon in the eleventh house; her Mars was widely conjunct her Ascendant, and the ruler of her Ascendant and her Moon was in Scorpio. Another example of a mother with problems centering round a child has South Moon in Leo in the twelfth house. She is hoping that psychiatric counseling now under way will help her daughter to live without drugs.

The more critical problems seem to follow the south node in the fifth house, or in Leo, other factors remaining equal. Its position in Aquarius or in the eleventh house strongly inclines toward a drive to gain knowledge and to give it to others, or to implement humanitarian principles, as in the well-known California yoga teacher, Jack Schwarz. But in the cases where the urge toward love and freedom are less well-integrated, it is common for this position of the lunar nodes to mean divorce and separation from children in the charts of males, with custody normally given to the mother. South Moon in Aquarius or in the eleventh house can also mean tensions and psychological discomfort in friendship, pointing to an individual who closes himself off to some extent. He may be critical of others and/or expect others to be critical of him, unless the chart shows warmth and acceptance in other ways. In extreme cases, the position may mark a real radical. On the positive side, unless the chart is an extremely difficult one, it indicates someone who is likely to be open to change and growth even though it may come in drastic upsets at times.

Virgo-Pisces or Sixth House-Twelfth House
These positions indicate a basic concern with health and healing which, when integrated, marks the doctor or other therapist and, when unresolved, marks the patient. Of the charts of medical doctors and psychotherapists available at this writing, a large proportion have their lunar nodes in either these signs or these houses,

and at times both are involved. Next to this polarity, the Aries-Libra placement is most prominent and appears frequently. Among psychologists who also teach, the signs Gemini-Sagittarius and Leo-Aquarius appear often, while Taurus-Scorpio and Cancer-Capricorn are minimally represented. Among the interesting individuals whose lives centered around healing by less orthodox methods and who also have the nodes in Virgo-Pisces, we can list the great psychic diagnostician Edgar Cayce; the modern psychic and founder of his own religious group, Fred Kimball; and another of the few women who have founded an enduring religious body, Mary Baker Eddy. The beliefs propounded by the latter in Christian Science, of course, center round the concept of healing without recourse to medicine.

Among the examples of individuals who are struggling to gain their own health, a set of twins with Virgo-Pisces nodes exemplifies the difference that can occur in a few minutes. In this case, one twin lived though he has been plagued by recurrent health problems throughout his life. His twin sister born just seventeen minutes later with the Moon exactly on the Midheaven was stillborn. The Moon ruled the Cancer Ascendant of both, and in the female chart its position exactly on the angle, which is ruled naturally by Saturn, showed the conditions beyond the control of the individual. (There is mounting evidence to suggest that the house cusps or dividing lines may have an effect much like the planets that are their natural rulers; e.g., Midheaven like Saturn, Ascendant like Mars, eleventh house cusp like Uranus, etc. In view of the controversy over differing house systems, research into this area is urgently needed.) Another example of Virgo-Pisces nodes foreshadowing health problems comes from the child already mentioned who died in infancy.

A differing challenge may appear in this nodal axis in relation to the sixth house association with one's work. The polar opposition of the nodes with the tendency to pull apart, added to the Virgo-Pisces search for perfection, often marks the individual with this placement as a job-hopper. At the least, the position indicates someone who requires variety in his work, and if the signs Virgo-Pisces fall in air-fire houses or the nodes in air-fire signs fall in the sixth-twelfth houses, there may be constant changes in the area of work. As always, the context of the whole chart must be read, and conservative or anxious qualities shown elsewhere may keep an individual in a job even though she or he would like to change.

Personal problems with health, or the choice of healing as an occupation, seem equally possible with either node on either side of this polarity. Charts of doctors as well as cases of health problems seem equally divided between the south node on the Virgo or on the Pisces side. While Virgo symbolizes the area of health, Pisces signifies hospitals or other institutions and the state of confinement resulting from loss of health, or it may indicate service to others in such states. This polarity brings into confrontation the Virgo passion for taking the world apart in order to make it run more efficiently and the Pisces search for union with the whole and the inner peace found through this sense of connectedness of life. When successfully integrated, this nodal axis represents a deep dedication to the wellbeing of humanity. The Pisces-Virgo person, especially if flavored with a little Cancer, can be the savior-martyr of the zodiac.

The third alternative to the savior-victim choice for this polarity is the artist-craftsperson. As the key to our search for the "emotional absolute," for infinite love and beauty, Pisces can mark the great creative artist while Virgo symbolizes the care with details of the artisan who does a good job for the sake of doing a good job. Whether we function as artist or as savior, integration involves work to bring the vision of a perfect world into tangible form.

Chapter 5

Summing Up

The failure of modern science to investigate the theories of astrology has, until recently, left the field largely in the hands of uneducated people who have continued to use and to teach the traditions handed down from the past. This situation is now beginning to change as research in astrology becomes more acceptable, but until such time as the basic principles can be validated, all statements about astrology must be considered hypotheses to be tested. This book is no exception. It offers much that is speculative and suggestive, but little can be pronounced as final truth. The principle points might be summed up as follows:

1. Correspondences exist between the patterns of the sky and events on Earth, but the reasons for the correspondences are still largely unknown, and it would be wise to avoid premature closure within a theoretical structure that might limit attention to possible areas of correspondence.

2. One such possible area of meaningful correspondence may appear in the sign and house positions and in the aspects of the geocentric nodes of the planets.

3. Preliminary work with these positions suggests that they carry the same qualities that have been found associated with their respective planets, with the north node normally indicating a point of receptivity and greater ease; the south node suggesting a point of stress and an obligation to learn and to release.

4. Research to date suggests that usually the nodes add emphasis and focus rather than new knowledge, but in many cases they seem to mark the difference between a relatively average individual and one with special talents or critical problems. They often mark individuals who will have an impact on the world and will reach a position of prominence and power.

5. One final reminder: Every factor of a chart must be considered in the context of the whole chart.

6. Research is needed. It is time for the academic world to take a serious look at astrology.

Node Tables
Planets

Geocentric Nodes of the Planets for every
even degree of the Sun's longitude.

Positions for 1950, with variations for one century.

Directions for Use

The nodes are given for every even degree of the Sun's longitude. Interpolate to the minute of the natal Sun where there is enough motion to warrant it. Each node is given in terms of degree, sign, minute, and variation for one century. The zodiacal position is given for 1950. The variation is the difference between the node position for 1900 and for 2000, when the Sun was at the same even degree. The variation is given in minutes of longitude. If the variation is positive, the position of the node is getting later in the zodiac in later years. If the variation is negative, the node is moving backward through the zodiac. Both the zodiacal sign and the variation are printed only when they change. If there is nothing in the sign or variation column for the Sun degree you are looking up, look up the column until there is an entrythat entry is still in effect.

For all dates, determine the number of years away from 1950, then divide this by 100. For your convenience, we have included a table giving this difference from 1950 divided by 100 on page 61. This number, multiplied by the variation given in the book for one century, gives the variation from 1950 to the year of interest. If the date is before 1950, subtract the variation from 1950 just obtained from the 1950 zodiacal positions given in the book. If the date is after 1950, add the variation from 1950 to the position in the book. Remember, since the variation can be positive or negative, you will sometimes be subtracting a negative number (which is the same as adding) and sometimes adding a negative number (which is the same as subtracting).

To give a more concrete example, Jimmy Carter was born in 1924, and his Sun is at 8 Libra 4. The nodes of Mercury, from the table, are:

Sun	North	V	South	V
8 ♎	23 ♍ 11	-17	20 ♎ 06	20
9 ♎	24 ♍ 25	-17	20 ♎ 49	20

I have filled in the blanks the table leaves for repeated entries in the sign and variation columns. To interpolate to 8 Libra 4, we want to go 4/60ths of the way from 8 to 9 Libra. 4/60 = .0666 . . . so we multiply the difference between listed positions by .0666 and add this to the 8 Libra positions. 24:25-23:11 = 1:14 = 74' x .0666 = 5' + 23:11 = 23 Virgo 16. 20:49 - 20:6 = 43' x .0666 = 3' + 20:6 = 20 Libra 9. Neither variation changes between 8 and 9 Libra Sun positions, so no interpolation is necessary for them. The difference between 1924 and 1950 divided by 100 is .26 (Table 3, page 61). The variations for a century times the fraction of a century are: -17 x .26 = -5 and 20 x .26 = 5. The positions of the nodes of Mercury for Jimmy Carter are: 23 Virgo 16 - -5 = 23 Virgo 21 for the north node and 20 Libra 9 - 5 = 20 Libra 4 for the south node.

For another example, on July 4, 1984 at 0 AM EDT the Sun will be at 12 Cancer 22. The nodes of Venus, from the table, are:

Sun	North	V	South	V
12 ♋	01 ♋ 21	22	23 ♌ 02	-32
13 ♋	01 ♋ 56	22	24 ♌ 36	-30

Our fraction for interpolating is 22/60 = .3666. North node: 1:56 -1:21 = 35 x .3666 = 13' + 1:21 = 1 Cancer 34. South node: 24:36 - 23:2 = 1:34 = 94 x .3666 = 34' + 23:2 = 23 Leo 36. The variation for the north node doesn't change, so no interpolation is necessary. The variation for the south node changes by 2 minutes, so: 2 x .3666 = 1 + -32 = -31. The difference between 1950 and 1984 divided by 100 is .34 (Table 3). The variations times the fraction of a century are: 22 x .34 = 7 and -31 x .34 = -11. The nodes of Venus for July 4,1984 are: 1 Cancer 34 + 7 = 1 Cancer 41 for the north node and 23 Leo 36 + -11 = 23 Leo 25 for the south node.

In these examples the answers have all been rounded to the

nearest minute. This can sometimes cause an error of a minute in the final result, but avoids giving an appearance of accuracy which is not really present.

Fewer steps may be necessary if the Sun is close to an even degree or the variation is small or the date is near 1950. However, this table structure does permit more accurate determination of the nodes than in our first edition.

It is possible for nodes, just like planets, to go retrograde.

This doesn't affect the procedures described here except that you need to be sure you subtract your motion from your earlier position.

Table 1, Astrological Symbols

	Signs		*Planets*		*Asteroids*
♈	Aries	☉	Sun	⚳	Ceres
♉	Taurus	☽	Moon	⚴	Pallas
♊	Gemini	☿	Mercury	⚵	Juno
♋	Cancer	♀	Venus	⚶	Vesta
♌	Leo	♂	Mars		
♍	Virgo	♃	Jupiter		*Others*
♎	Libra	♄	Saturn	NN	North Node
♏	Scorpio	♅	Uranus	SN	South Node
♐	Sagittari us	♆	Neptune	V	Variation
♑	Capricorn	♇	Pluto		
♒	Aquarius				
♓	Pisces				

Table 2, Heliocentric North Node

Date	☿		♀		♂		♃	
1/1/1850	16 ♉ 33		15 ♊ 20		18 ♉ 24		08 ♋ 56	
1/1/1900	17	09	15	47	18	47	09	02
1/1/1950	17	44	16	14	19	10	09	57
1/1/2000	18	20	16	41	19	33	10	27
1/1/2050	18	56	17	08	19	57	10	59

Date	♄		♅		♆		♀	
1/1/1850	22 ♋ 21		13 ♊ 14		10 ♌ 08		18 ♋ 15	
1/1/1900	22	47	13	29	10	41	18	57
1/1/1950	23	13	13	45	11	14	19	38
1/1/2000	23	39	14	00	11	47	20	19
1/1/2050	24	06	14	16	12	20	20	59

Date	?		☿		✳		⚼	
1/1/1850	20 ♊ 30		22 ♍ 46		21 ♍ 21		13 ♋ 09	
1/1/1900	20	40	22	52	20	47	13	33
1/1/1950	20	43	23	01	20	27	13	52
1/1/2000	20	39	23	14	20	23	14	08
1/1/2050	20	35	23	32	20	16	14	22

Table 3, Fraction of Century 1850-2000

1850	1.00	1900	.50	1950	.00
1851	.99	1901	.49	1951	.01
1852	.98	1902	.48	1952	.02
1853	.97	1903	.47	1953	.03
1854	.96	1904	.46	1954	.04
1855	.95	1905	.45	1955	.05
1856	.94	1906	.44	1956	.06
1857	.93	1907	.43	1957	.07
1858	.92	1908	.42	1958	.08
1859	.91	1909	.41	1959	.09
1860	.90	1910	.40	1960	.10
1861	.89	1911	.39	1961	.11
1862	.88	1912	.38	1962	.12
1863	.87	1913	.37	1963	.13
1864	.86	1914	.36	1964	.14
1865	.85	1915	.35	1965	.15
1866	.84	1916	.34	1966	.16
1867	.83	1917	.33	1967	.17
1868	.82	1918	.32	1968	.18
1869	.81	1919	.31	1969	.19
1870	.80	1920	.30	1970	.20
1871	.79	1921	.29	1971	.21
1872	.78	1922	.28	1972	.22
1873	.77	1923	.27	1973	.23
1874	.76	1924	.26	1974	.24
1875	.75	1925	.25	1975	.25
1876	.74	1926	.24	1976	.26
1877	.73	1927	.23	1977	.27
1878	.72	1928	.22	1978	.28
1879	.71	1929	.21	1979	.29
1880	.70	1930	.20	1980	.30
1881	.69	1931	.19	1981	.31
1882	.68	1932	.18	1982	.32
1883	.67	1933	.17	1983	.33
1884	.66	1934	.16	1984	.34
1885	.65	1935	.15	1985	.35
1886	.64	1936	.14	1986	.36
1887	.63	1937	.13	1987	.37
1888	.62	1938	.12	1988	.38
1889	.61	1939	.11	1989	.39
1890	.60	1940	.10	1990	.40
1891	.59	1941	.09	1991	.41
1892	.58	1942	.08	1992	.42
1893	.57	1943	.07	1993	.43
1894	.56	1944	.06	1994	.44
1895	.55	1945	.05	1995	.45
1896	.54	1946	.04	1996	.46
1897	.53	1947	.03	1997	.47
1898	.52	1948	.02	1998	.48
1899	.51	1949	.01	1999	.49
1900	.50	1950	.00	2000	.50

Table 3, Fraction of Century 2000-2100

Year	Value	Year	Value
2000	.50	2050	.00
2001	.49	2051	.01
2002	.48	2052	.02
2003	.47	2053	.03
2004	.46	2054	.04
2005	.45	2055	.05
2006	.44	2056	.06
2007	.43	2057	.07
2008	.42	2058	.08
2009	.41	2059	.09
2010	.40	2060	.10
2011	.39	2061	.11
2012	.38	2062	.12
2013	.37	2063	.13
2014	.36	2064	.14
2015	.35	2065	.15
2016	.34	2066	.16
2017	.33	2067	.17
2018	.32	2068	.18
2019	.31	2069	.19
2020	.30	2070	.20
2021	.29	2071	.21
2022	.28	2072	.22
2023	.27	2073	.23
2024	.26	2074	.24
2025	.25	2075	.25
2026	.24	2076	.26
2027	.23	2077	.27
2028	.22	2078	.28
2029	.21	2079	.29
2030	.20	2080	.30
2031	.19	2081	.31
2032	.18	2082	.32
2033	.17	2083	.33
2034	.16	2084	.34
2035	.15	2085	.35
2036	.14	2086	.36
2037	.13	2087	.37
2038	.12	2088	.38
2039	.11	2089	.39
2040	.10	2090	.40
2041	.09	2091	.41
2042	.08	2092	.42
2043	.07	2093	.43
2044	.06	2094	.44
2045	.05	2095	.45
2046	.04	2096	.46
2047	.03	2097	.47
2048	.02	2098	.48
2049	.01	2099	.49
2050	.00	2100	.50

☉	☿ NN	V	☿ SN	V	♀ NN	V	♀ SN	V
00 ♈	10 ♈54	15	04 ♓12	-11	00 ♉56	21	19 ♒25	15
01	11 42		05 23	-12	01 33		20 08	
02	12 29		06 35	-13	02 10		20 51	
03	13 16		07 47	-14	02 47		21 34	
04	14 04		09 01	-15	03 24		22 17	14
05	14 51		10 15	-16	04 01		23 01	
06	15 38	16	11 30	-17	04 38		23 45	
07	16 25		12 46	-18	05 15		24 30	13
08	17 12		14 03	-20	05 52		25 14	
09	17 59		15 21	-21	06 28		25 59	
10	18 46		16 40	-22	07 05		26 45	12
11	19 33		18 00	-23	07 41		27 31	
12	20 19		19 21	-24	08 18	22	28 17	
13	21 06		20 43	-25	08 54		29 04	11
14	21 53		22 05	-26	09 31		29 51	
15	22 39		23 29	-28	10 07		00 ♓39	10
16	23 26		24 54	-29	10 43		01 27	
17	24 12		26 20	-30	11 19		02 16	
18	24 58		27 47	-31	11 55		03 05	09
19	25 45		29 15	-33	12 31		03 55	
20	26 31		00 ♈44	-34	13 07		04 45	08
21	27 17	17	02 14	-35	13 43		05 36	07
22	28 04		03 45	-36	14 19		06 28	
23	28 50		05 17	-38	14 55		07 20	06
24	29 36		06 50	-39	15 31		08 13	
25	00 ♉22		08 24	-40	16 07		09 06	05
26	01 08		10 00	-41	16 43		10 01	04
27	01 54		11 36	-43	17 18		10 56	03
28	02 40		13 13	-44	17 54		11 52	
29	03 26		14 51	-45	18 30		12 49	02
00 ♉	04 12		16 31	-46	19 05		13 47	01
01	04 58		18 11	-47	19 41		14 46	00
02	05 44		19 52	-48	20 17		15 46	-01
03	06 30		21 34	-49	20 52		16 47	-02
04	07 15		23 16	-50	21 28		17 49	-03
05	08 01		25 00	-51	22 03		18 53	-04
06	08 47		26 44	-52	22 39		19 57	-06
07	09 33		28 29	-53	23 14		21 03	-07
08	10 19		00 ♉15	-54	23 50		22 11	-08
09	11 05		02 01	-55	24 25		23 20	-10
10	11 50		03 47		25 00		24 30	-11
11	12 36		05 34	-56	25 36		25 43	-13
12	13 22		07 22		26 11		26 57	-14
13	14 08		09 10	-57	26 46		28 13	-16
14	14 53		10 58		27 22		29 31	-18
15	15 39		12 47		27 57		00 ♈52	-20
16	16 25		14 35	-58	28 32		02 14	-22
17	17 11		16 24		29 07		03 39	-24
18	17 56		18 13		29 43		05 07	-27
19	18 42		20 01		00 ♊18		06 37	-29
20	19 28		21 50	-57	00 53		08 11	-32
21	20 14		23 38		01 28		09 47	-35
22	20 59		25 26		02 03		11 27	-38

☉	♂ NN	V	♂ SN	V	♃ NN	V	♃ SN	V
00 ♈	29 ♈ 38	28	29 ♐ 09	40	28 ♊ 51	60	20 ♑ 17	56
01	00 ♉ 01		29 09	41	28 51		20 21	
02	00 24		29 08	42	28 51		20 25	57
03	00 47		29 06		28 52		20 28	
04	01 10	27	29 02	43	28 53		20 32	
05	01 33		28 58	44	28 54	59	20 35	
06	01 56		28 52	45	28 55		20 38	
07	02 19		28 46		28 56		20 41	
08	02 43		28 38	46	28 58		20 44	58
09	03 06		28 29	47	28 59		20 46	
10	03 29		28 18	48	29 01	58	20 49	
11	03 53		28 07	49	29 03		20 51	
12	04 16		27 53	50	29 06		20 53	
13	04 40		27 38	51	29 08		20 55	
14	05 03		27 22	53	29 11		20 56	59
15	05 27		27 03	54	29 13		20 58	
16	05 50		26 43	55	29 16	57	20 59	
17	05 14		26 21	57	29 19		21 00	
18	06 38		25 57	58	29 23		21 01	
19	07 01		25 31	60	29 26		21 02	60
20	07 25		25 03	61	29 30		21 02	
21	07 49		24 33	63	29 34		21 03	
22	08 13		24 00	65	29 38	56	21 03	
23	08 37		23 24	67	29 42		21 03	
24	09 01		22 46	69	29 46		21 02	61
25	09 25		22 06	71	29 50		21 02	
26	09 49		21 22	73	29 55		21 01	
27	10 13		20 35	76	00 ♋ 00		21 00	
28	10 37		19 46	78	00 04		20 59	
29	11 01		18 53	81	00 09	55	20 56	62
00 ♉	11 25		17 57	83	00 14		20 56	
01	11 49		16 57	86	00 20		20 54	
02	12 13		15 54	89	00 25		20 52	
03	12 37		14 47	92	00 31		20 50	63
04	13 01		13 37	95	00 36		20 47	
05	13 26		12 23	98	00 42		20 45	
06	13 50		11 05	101	00 48	54	20 42	
07	14 14		09 44	104	00 54		20 38	64
08	14 38		08 19	107	01 00		20 35	
09	15 03		06 50	111	01 07		20 31	
10	15 27		05 18	114	01 13		20 27	
11	15 51		03 43	116	01 20		20 23	65
12	16 16		02 04	119	01 26		20 19	
13	16 40		00 23	122	01 33		20 14	
14	17 04		28 ♏ 38	124	01 40		20 09	
15	17 29		26 52	127	01 47	53	20 04	66
16	17 53		25 03	129	01 54		19 59	
17	18 17		23 13	130	02 01		19 53	
18	18 42		21 22	132	02 08		19 47	
19	19 06		19 30	133	02 16		19 41	67
20	19 31		17 38		02 23		19 35	
21	19 55		15 46		02 31		19 28	
22	20 19	28	13 55		02 38		19 21	

☉	♄ NN	V	♄ SN	V	♅ NN	V	♅ SN	V
00 ♈	17 ♋ 11	54	28 ♑ 15	50	10 ♊ 56	30	16 ♐ 40	31
01	17 09		28 17		10 57		16 39	
02	17 07		28 20		10 58		16 38	
03	17 05		28 23		11 00		16 38	
04	17 03		28 25		11 01		16 37	
05	17 02		28 27		11 02		16 36	
06	17 00		28 30		11 03		16 35	
07	16 59		28 32		11 04		16 34	
08	16 57	53	28 34		11 06		16 33	
09	16 56		28 36		11 07		16 31	
10	16 55		28 38	51	11 08		16 30	
11	16 55		28 40		11 10		16 29	
12	16 54		28 42		11 11		16 28	
13	16 53		28 44		11 13		16 26	
14	16 53		28 45		11 14		16 25	
15	16 52		28 47		11 16		16 23	32
16	16 52		28 48		11 18		16 22	
17	16 52		28 50		11 19		16 20	
18	16 52	52	28 51		11 21		16 19	
19	16 52		28 52		11 23		16 17	
20	16 52		28 53		11 25		16 15	
21	16 52		28 54		11 27		16 13	
22	16 53		28 55	52	11 29		16 12	
23	16 53		28 56		11 31		16 10	
24	16 54		28 56		11 32		16 08	
25	16 55		28 57		11 35		16 06	
26	16 56		28 58		11 37		16 04	
27	16 57		28 58		11 39		16 02	
28	16 58	51	28 58		11 41		16 00	
29	16 59		28 58		11 43		15 57	
00 ♉	17 00		28 58		11 45		15 55	
01	17 02		28 58		11 47		15 53	
02	17 03		28 58		11 50		15 51	
03	17 05		28 58	53	11 52		15 48	
04	17 07		28 57		11 54		15 46	
05	17 08		28 57		11 57		15 43	
06	17 10		28 56		11 59		15 41	
07	17 12		28 56		12 02		15 38	
08	17 15		28 55		12 04	29	15 36	
09	17 17	50	28 54		12 06		15 33	
10	17 19		28 53		12 09		15 30	
11	17 22		28 52		12 12		15 28	
12	17 24		28 50		12 14		15 25	
13	17 27		28 49	54	12 17		15 22	
14	17 30		28 48		12 19		15 19	
15	17 32		28 46		12 22		15 17	
16	17 35		28 44		12 25		15 14	
17	17 38		28 42		12 27		15 11	
18	17 41		28 40		12 30		15 08	
19	17 45		28 38		12 33		15 05	
20	17 48		28 36		12 35		15 02	
21	17 51	49	28 34		12 38		14 59	
22	17 55		28 32		12 41		14 56	

☉	Ψ NN	V	Ψ SN	V	♀ NN	V	♀ SN	V
00 ♈	09 ♌ 46	68	12 ♒38	65	18 ♋19	83	21 ♑13	82
01	09 45		12 39		18 19		21 13	
02	09 44		12 40		18 18		21 14	
03	09 42	67	12 42		18 18		21 15	
04	09 41		12 43		18 17		21 15	
05	09 40		12 44		18 17		21 16	
06	09 39		12 45		18 17		21 16	
07	09 38		12 47		18 16		21 17	
08	09 37		12 48		18 16		21 17	
09	09 36		12 49		18 16		21 18	
10	09 34		12 50		18 16		21 18	
11	09 33		12 51		18 15		21 18	
12	09 32		12 52		18 15		21 19	
13	09 32		12 53		18 15		21 19	
14	09 31		12 54		18 15		21 19	
15	09 30		12 55		18 15		21 20	
16	09 29		12 56		18 15		21 20	
17	09 28		12 57		18 15		21 20	83
18	09 27		12 58		18 15		21 20	
19	09 27		12 59		18 14		21 20	
20	09 26		12 59		18 15	82	21 20	
21	09 25		13 00		18 15		21 20	
22	09 24		13 01		18 15		21 20	
23	09 24		13 02		18 15		21 20	
24	09 23		13 02		18 15		21 20	
25	09 23		13 03		18 15		21 20	
26	09 22		13 04		18 15		21 20	
27	09 22		13 04		18 15		21 20	
28	09 21		13 05		18 16		21 20	
29	09 21		13 05	66	18 16		21 20	
00 ♉	09 20		13 06		18 16		21 19	
01	09 20	66	13 06		18 16		21 19	
02	09 20		13 07		18 17		21 19	
03	09 20		13 07		18 17		21 19	
04	09 20		13 08		18 17		21 18	
05	09 19		13 08		18 18		21 18	
06	09 19		13 08		18 18		21 17	
07	09 19		13 08		18 19		21 17	
08	09 19		13 08		18 19		21 16	
09	09 19		13 09		18 19		21 16	
10	09 19		13 09		18 20		21 15	84
11	09 19		13 09		18 21		21 15	
12	09 19		13 09		18 21		21 14	
13	09 19		13 09		18 22		21 14	
14	09 19		13 09		18 22		21 13	
15	09 19		13 09		18 23		21 12	
16	09 19		13 09		18 24		21 12	
17	09 20		13 09		18 24		21 11	
18	09 20		13 09		18 25		21 10	
19	09 20		13 09		18 26	81	21 09	
20	09 20		13 09		18 26		21 08	
21	09 21		13 08		18 27		21 08	
22	09 21		13 08		18 28		21 07	

☉	☿ NN	V	☿ SN	V	♀ NN	V	♀ NN	V
22 ♉	20 ♉ 59	17	25 ♉ 26	-57	02 ♊ 03	22	11 ♈ 27	-38
23	21 45		27 14	-56	02 39		13 11	-41
24	22 31		29 01		03 14	23	14 58	-45
25	23 17		00 ♊ 48	-55	03 49		16 49	-48
26	24 03		02 34		04 24	22	18 44	-52
27	24 49		04 20	-54	04 59		20 44	-57
28	25 35		06 05		05 34		22 49	-61
29	26 20		07 49	-53	06 09		24 58	-65
00 ♊	27 06		09 33	-52	06 44		27 12	-70
01	27 52		11 16	-51	07 20		29 32	-75
02	28 38	16	12 58	-50	07 55		01 ♉ 58	-80
03	29 24		14 39	-49	08 30		04 29	-85
04	00 ♊ 10		16 20	-48	09 05		07 07	-91
05	00 56		17 59	-47	09 40		09 50	-96
06	01 43		19 38	-46	10 15		12 39	-102
07	02 29		21 15	-45	10 50		15 34	-107
08	03 15		22 52	-44	11 25		18 35	-112
09	04 01		24 28	-43	12 00		21 42	-117
10	04 47		26 02	-41	12 35		24 54	-121
11	05 34		27 36	-40	13 10		28 11	-125
12	06 20		29 08	-39	13 45		01 ♊ 32	-129
13	07 06		00 ♋ 40	-38	14 21		04 57	-132
14	07 53		02 10	-37	14 56		08 24	-134
15	08 53		03 40	-35	14 56		08 54	-135
16	09 26		05 08	-34	16 06		15 25	-136
17	10 12		06 36	-33	16 41		18 55	
18	10 56		08 02	-32	17 16		22 25	-134
19	11 46		09 27	-31	17 51		25 53	-132
20	12 33	15	10 52	-29	18 26		29 19	-129
21	13 19		12 15	-28	19 01		02 ♋ 41	-126
22	14 06		13 37	-27	19 36		05 58	-122
23	14 53		14 59	-26	20 12		09 11	-117
24	15 40		16 19	-25	20 47		12 19	-112
25	16 27		17 39	-24	21 22		15 21	-107
26	17 15		18 57	-23	21 57		18 18	-102
27	18 02		20 15	-22	22 32		21 08	-97
28	18 49		21 31	-21	21 07		23 53	-91
29	19 36		22 47	-20	23 43		26 31	-86
00 ♋	20 24		24 02	-19	24 18		29 03	-81
01	21 11	14	25 16	-18	24 53		01 ♌ 30	-75
02	21 59		26 29	-17	25 28		03 51	-71
03	22 47		27 42	-16	26 03		06 07	-66
04	23 35		28 53	-15	26 39		08 17	-61
05	24 22		00 ♌ 04	-14	27 14		10 22	-57
06	25 10		01 14	-13	27 49		12 23	-53
07	25 58		02 23	-12	28 24		14 19	-49
08	26 47		03 32	-11	29 00		16 11	-45
09	27 35		04 40	-10	29 35		17 59	-42
10	28 23	13	05 47	-09	00 ♋ 10		19 44	-38
11	29 12		06 54		00 46		21 24	-35
12	00 ♋ 00		07 59	-08	01 21		23 02	-32
13	00 49		09 05	-07	01 56		24 36	-30
14	01 38		10 09	-06	02 32		26 07	-27

☉	♂ NN		V	♂ SN		V	♃ NN		V	♃ SN		V
22 ♉	20 ♉	19	28	13 ♏	55	133	02 ♋	38	53	19 ♑	21	67
23	20	44		12	05		02	46		19	14	68
24	21	08		10	16	132	02	54		19	07	
25	21	33		08	30	131	03	02	52	18	59	
26	21	57		06	45	130	03	10		18	51	
27	22	22		05	04	128	03	18		18	43	69
28	22	46		03	25	126	03	26		18	35	
29	23	11		01	50	124	03	35		18	26	
00 ♊	23	35		00	18	122	03	43		18	18	
01	23	59		28 ♎	49	119	03	51		18	09	70
02	24	24		27	24	117	04	00		17	59	
03	24	48		26	03	114	04	08		17	50	
04	25	13		24	45	112	04	17		17	40	
05	25	37		23	31	109	04	26		17	30	
06	26	01		22	21	106	04	34		17	20	71
07	26	26		21	15	103	04	43		17	10	
08	26	50		20	12	101	04	52		16	59	
09	27	14		19	12	98	05	01	51	16	48	
10	27	39		18	17	96	05	10		16	37	72
11	28	03		17	24	93	05	19		16	26	
12	28	27		16	34	91	05	28		16	15	
13	28	52		15	48	88	05	37		16	03	
14	29	16		15	05	86	05	47		15	51	
15	29	40		14	24	84	05	56		15	39	73
16	00 ♊	05		13	47	82	06	05		15	27	
17	00	29		13	11	80	06	14		15	14	
18	00	53		12	39	78	06	24		15	02	
19	01	17		12	09	76	06	33		14	49	
20	01	41		11	41	74	06	43		14	36	74
21	02	05		11	15	72	06	52		14	23	
22	02	30		10	52	71	07	02		14	10	
23	02	54	29	10	30	69	07	11		13	57	
24	03	18		10	10	67	07	21		13	43	
25	03	42		09	52	66	07	31		13	30	
26	04	06		09	36	65	07	40		13	16	
27	04	30		09	22	63	07	50		13	02	75
28	04	53		09	09	62	08	00		12	48	
29	05	17		08	57	61	08	09		12	34	
00 ♋	05	41		08	48	60	08	19		12	20	
01	06	05		08	39	58	08	29		12	06	
02	06	29		08	32	57	08	39		11	52	
03	06	52		08	25	56	08	49		11	38	
04	07	16		08	21	55	08	58		11	23	
05	07	40		08	17	54	09	08		11	09	
06	08	03		08	14		09	18		10	54	
07	08	27		08	12	53	09	28		10	40	
08	08	50		08	12	52	09	38		10	25	
09	09	14		08	12	51	09	48		10	11	
10	09	37	30	08	13	50	09	57		09	56	
11	10	00		08	15	49	10	07		09	42	
12	10	23		08	18		10	17		09	27	
13	10	47		08	21	48	10	27		09	13	
14	11	10		08	26	47	10	37		08	58	

☉	♄ NN	V	♄ SN	V	♅ NN	V	♅ SN	V
22 ♉	17 ♋ 55	49	28 ♑ 32	54	12 ♊ 41	29	14 ♐ 56	32
23	17 58		28 29	55	12 44		14 53	
24	18 02		28 26		12 47		14 50	
25	18 05		28 24		12 50		14 47	
26	18 09		28 21		12 52		14 43	
27	18 13		28 18		12 55		14 40	
28	18 17		28 15		12 58		14 37	
29	18 21		28 12		13 01		14 34	
00 ♊	18 25		28 08		13 04		14 31	
01	18 29		28 05		13 07		14 27	
02	18 33		28 02		13 10		14 24	
03	18 42		27 58		13 13		14 21	
04	18 42		27 54	56	13 16		14 18	
05	18 47		27 50		13 19		14 14	
06	18 51	48	27 47		13 22		14 11	
07	18 56		27 43		13 25		14 08	
08	19 00		27 38		13 28		14 04	
09	19 05		27 34		13 31		14 01	
10	19 10		27 30		13 34		13 57	
11	19 14		27 26		13 37		13 54	
12	19 19		27 21		13 40		13 51	
13	19 24		27 16		13 43		13 47	
14	19 29		27 12		13 46		13 44	
15	19 34		27 07	57	13 49		13 41	
16	19 39		27 02		13 52		13 37	
17	19 45		26 57		13 55		13 34	
18	19 50		26 52		13 58		13 30	
19	19 55		26 47		14 01		13 27	
20	20 00		26 42		14 04		13 24	
21	20 06		26 36		14 07		13 20	
22	20 11		26 31		14 10		13 17	
23	20 16		26 25		14 13		13 14	
24	20 22		26 20		14 16		13 10	
25	20 27		26 14		14 19		13 07	
26	20 33		26 08		14 21		13 04	
27	20 38		26 03		14 24		13 01	
28	20 44	47	25 57	58	14 27		12 57	
29	20 50		25 51		14 30		12 54	
00 ♋	20 55		25 45		14 33		12 51	
01	21 01		25 39		14 36		12 48	
02	21 07		25 33		14 39		12 44	
03	21 13		25 26		14 42		12 41	
04	21 18		25 20		14 45		12 38	
05	21 24		25 14		14 48		12 35	
06	21 30		25 08		14 50		12 32	
07	21 36		25 01		14 53		12 29	
08	21 42		24 55		14 56		12 26	
09	21 48		24 48		14 59		12 23	
10	21 54		24 42		15 02		12 20	
11	22 00		24 35		15 04		12 17	
12	22 06		24 29		15 07		12 14	
13	22 12		24 22		15 10		12 11	
14	22 18		24 16		15 12		12 08	

☉	Ψ NN	V	Ψ SN	V	♀ NN	V	♀ SN	V
22 ♉	09 ♌ 21	66	13 ♒ 08	66	18 ♋ 28	81	21 ♑ 07	84
23	09 22		13 08		18 29		21 06	
24	09 22		13 08		18 29		21 05	
25	09 23		13 07	67	18 30		21 04	
26	09 23		13 07		18 31		21 03	
27	09 24	65	13 06		18 32		21 02	
28	09 24		13 06		18 33		21 01	
29	09 24		13 05		18 34		21 00	
00 ♊	09 25		13 05		18 35		20 58	
01	09 26		13 04		18 36		20 57	
02	09 27		13 04		18 37		20 56	
03	09 28		13 03		18 38		20 55	
04	09 29		13 02		18 39		20 54	
05	09 29		13 01		18 40		20 52	
06	09 30		13 01		18 41		20 51	
07	09 31		13 00		18 42		20 50	
08	09 32		12 59		18 43		20 48	85
09	09 33		12 58		18 44		20 47	
10	09 34		12 57		18 45		20 46	
11	09 35		12 56		18 46		20 44	
12	09 36		12 55		18 48		20 43	
13	09 37		12 54		18 49		20 41	
14	09 38		12 53		18 50		20 40	
15	09 39		12 52		18 51		20 39	
16	09 40		12 51		18 52		20 37	
17	09 42		12 50		18 53		20 36	
18	09 43		12 49		18 55		20 34	
19	09 44		12 48		18 56		20 32	
20	09 45		12 47		18 57		20 31	
21	09 47		12 45		18 58		20 29	
22	09 48		12 44	68	19 00		20 28	
23	09 49		12 43		19 01		20 26	
24	09 51		12 41		19 02		20 24	
25	09 52		12 40		19 04		20 23	
26	09 53		12 39		19 05		20 21	
27	09 55		12 37		19 06		20 19	
28	09 56		12 36		19 08		20 18	
29	09 58	64	12 34		19 09		20 16	
00 ♋	09 59		12 33		19 10		20 14	
01	10 01		12 31		19 12		20 12	
02	10 02		12 30		19 13		20 11	
03	10 04		12 28		19 15		20 09	
04	10 06		12 26		19 16		20 07	
05	10 07		12 25		19 17		20 05	
06	10 09		12 23		19 19		20 03	
07	10 10		12 21		19 20		20 02	
08	10 12		12 20		19 22	80	20 00	
09	10 14		12 18		19 23		19 58	
10	10 15		12 16		19 24		19 56	
11	10 17		12 14		19 26		19 54	
12	10 19		12 13		19 27		19 ♑ 52	
13	10 21		12 11		19 29		19 51	
14	10 22		12 09		19 30		19 49	

☉	☿ NN		☿ SN		♀ NN		♀ SN	
		V		V		V		V
14 ♋	01 ♋38	13	10 ♌09	-06	02 ♋32	22	26 ♌07	-27
15	02 21		11 13		03 07		27 35	-25
16	03 16		12 16	-05	03 43		29 01	-22
17	04 05	12	13 19	-04	04 18		00 ♍24	-20
18	04 54		14 21	-03	04 54		01 45	-18
19	05 44		15 23		05 29		03 04	-16
20	06 33		16 24	-02	06 05		04 21	-14
21	07 23		17 24		06 40		05 36	-13
22	08 13		18 24	-01	07 16		06 49	-11
23	09 02	11	19 24	00	07 51		08 00	-10
24	09 53		20 23		08 27		09 09	-08
25	10 43		21 21	01	09 03		10 17	-07
26	11 33		22 19		09 39		11 24	-06
27	12 24		23 17	02	10 14		12 29	-05
28	13 14		24 14		10 50		13 33	-03
29	14 05	10	25 11	03	11 26		14 36	-02
00 ♌	14 56		26 07		12 02		15 37	-01
01	15 47		27 03	04	12 37		16 38	00
02	16 38		27 59		13 13		17 37	01
03	17 30		28 54	05	13 49		18 36	
04	18 22	09	29 48		14 25		19 33	02
05	19 13		00 ♍43	06	15 01		20 30	03
06	20 05		01 37		15 37		21 25	04
07	20 58		02 30	07	16 13	21	22 20	
08	21 50		03 24		16 49	22	23 15	05
09	22 43	08	04 17		17 26	21	24 08	06
10	23 35		05 09	08	18 02		25 01	
11	24 28		06 02		18 38		25 53	07
12	25 21	07	06 54		19 14		26 44	08
13	26 15		07 46	09	19 51		27 35	
14	27 09		08 37		20 27		28 25	09
15	28 02		09 28	10	21 04		29 15	
16	28 56		10 19		21 40		00 ♎04	10
17	29 51	06	11 10	11	22 17		00 53	
18	00 ♌ 45		12 00		22 53		01 41	
19	01 40		12 50		23 30		02 29	11
20	02 35	05	13 40		24 07		03 16	
21	03 30		14 29	12	24 44		04 03	12
22	04 26		15 19		25 20		04 49	
23	05 21	04	16 08		25 57		05 35	
24	06 17		16 57		26 34		06 21	
25	07 14		17 45	13	27 11		07 06	13
26	08 10	03	18 34		27 48		07 51	
27	09 07		19 22		28 26		08 35	14
28	10 04		20 10		29 03	20	09 20	
29	11 02	02	20 58	14	29 40		10 04	
00 ♍	11 59		21 45		00 ♌ 18		10 47	
01	12 57		22 33		00 55		11 31	15
02	13 56	01	23 20		01 33		12 14	
03	14 54		24 07	15	02 11		12 57	
04	15 53		24 54		02 48		13 39	
05	16 53	00	25 41		03 26		14 21	
06	17 52		26 27		04 04		15 03	

☉	♂ NN	V	♂ SN	V	♃ NN	V	♃ SN	V
14 ♋	11 ♊ 10	30	08 ♎ 26	47	10 ♋ 37	51	08 ♑ 58	75
15	11 33		08 31		10 47		08 44	
16	11 56		08 36	46	10 56		08 29	
17	12 19		08 43		11 06		08 15	
18	12 42		08 50	45	11 16		08 00	
19	13 04		08 57		11 26		07 46	
20	13 27		09 06	44	11 36		07 32	
21	13 50	31	09 14		11 45		07 18	
22	14 12		09 24	43	11 55		07 04	
23	14 35		09 33		12 05		06 50	
24	14 57		09 44	42	12 15		06 36	
25	15 19		09 54		12 24		06 22	
26	15 41		10 06	41	12 34		06 09	74
27	16 04		10 17		12 43		05 55	
28	16 26		10 29		12 53		05 42	
29	16 47		10 42	40	13 03		05 29	
00 ♌	17 09		10 55		13 12		05 16	
01	17 31	32	11 08	39	13 22		05 03	
02	17 53		11 22		13 31		04 50	
03	18 14		11 36		13 40		04 38	73
04	18 35		11 50	38	13 50		04 25	
05	18 57		12 04		13 59		04 13	
06	19 18		12 19		14 08		04 01	
07	19 39		12 35		14 18		03 49	
08	20 00	33	12 50	37	14 27	52	03 38	
09	20 20		13 06		14 36		03 26	72
10	20 41		13 22		14 45		03 15	
11	21 01		13 38		14 54		03 04	
12	21 22		13 55	36	15 03		02 53	
13	21 42		14 12		15 12		02 43	71
14	22 02	34	14 29		15 21		02 32	
15	22 22		14 46		15 29		02 22	
16	22 41		15 04	35	15 38		02 12	
17	23 01		15 21		15 47		02 03	
18	23 20		15 39		15 55		01 53	70
19	23 39	35	15 57		16 04		01 44	
20	23 58		16 16		16 12		01 35	
21	24 17		16 34	34	16 20		01 26	
22	24 35		16 53		16 29	53	01 17	69
23	24 54		17 12		16 37		01 09	
24	25 12	36	17 31		16 45		01 01	
25	25 30		17 50		16 53		00 53	
26	25 47		18 09		17 01		00 46	68
27	26 05		18 29	33	17 09		00 38	
28	26 22	37	18 48		17 17		00 31	
29	26 39		19 08		17 24		00 24	
00 ♍	26 55		19 28		17 32		00 18	67
01	27 12		19 48		17 39		00 11	
02	27 28	38	20 08		17 47	54	00 05	
03	27 44		20 28	32	17 54		00 00	
04	27 59		20 49		17 01		29 ♐ 54	66
05	28 14	39	21 09		18 08		29 49	
06	28 29		21 30		18 15		29 43	

☉	♄ NN		V	♄ SN		V	♅ NN		V	♅ SN		V
14 ♋	22 ♋	18	47	24 ♑	16	58	15 ♊	12	29	12 ♐	08	32
15	22	24		24	09		15	15		12	05	
16	22	30		24	02		15	18		12	02	
17	22	36		23	55		15	20		12	00	
18	22	42		23	49		15	23		11	57	
19	22	48		23	42		15	25		11	54	
20	22	54		23	35		15	28		11	52	
21	23	00		23	29		15	30		11	49	
22	23	06		23	22		15	33		11	46	
23	23	12		23	15		15	35		11	44	
24	23	18		23	08		15	38		11	41	
25	23	24		23	01		15	40		11	39	
26	23	30		22	55		15	42		11	37	
27	23	36		22	48		15	45		11	34	
28	23	42		22	41		15	47		11	32	
29	23	48		22	35		15	49		11	30	
00 ♌	23	55		22	28		15	51		11	27	
01	24	01		22	21		15	54		11	25	
02	24	07		22	14		15	56		11	23	
03	24	13		22	08		15	58		11	21	
04	24	19		22	01		16	00		11	19	31
05	24	24		21	55		16	02	30	11	17	
06	24	30		21	48		16	04		11	15	
07	24	36		21	42		16	06		11	13	
08	24	42		21	35		16	08		11	12	
09	24	48		21	29		16	09		11	10	
10	24	54		21	22		16	11		11	08	
11	25	00		21	16		16	13		11	06	
12	25	06		21	10		16	15		11	05	
13	25	12		21	04		16	16		11	03	
14	25	17		20	57		16	18		11	02	
15	25	23		20	51		16	20		11	00	
16	25	29		20	45		16	21		10	59	
17	25	34		20	39		16	23		10	58	
18	25	40	48	20	33		16	24		10	56	
19	25	46		20	28	57	16	26		10	55	
20	25	51		20	22		16	27		10	54	
21	25	57		20	16		16	28		10	53	
22	26	02		20	10		16	30		10	52	
23	26	08		20	05		16	31		10	51	
24	26	13		19	59		16	32		10	50	
25	26	18		19	54		16	33		10	49	
26	26	24		19	49		16	34		10	48	
27	26	29		19	43		15	35		10	47	
28	26	34		19	38		16	36		10	47	
29	26	39		19	33		16	37		10	46	
00 ♍	26	45		19	28		16	38		10	46	
01	26	50		19	23		16	39		10	45	
02	26	55		19	19		16	40		10	45	
03	27	00		19	14	56	16	40		10	44	
04	27	05		19	09		16	41		10	44	
05	27	09		19	05		16	42		10	43	
06	27	14		19	00		16	42		10	43	

⊙	Ψ NN	V	Ψ SN	V	♀ NN	V	♀ SN	V
14 ♋	10 ♌ 22	64	12 ♒ 09	68	19 ♋ 30	80	19 ♑ 49	85
15	10 24		12 07		19 32		19 47	
16	10 26		12 05		19 33		19 45	
17	10 28		12 03		19 34		19 43	
18	10 30		12 01		19 36		19 41	
19	10 31		12 00		19 37		19 39	
20	10 33		11 58		19 39		19 38	
21	10 35		11 56		19 40		19 36	
22	10 37		11 54		19 42		19 34	
23	10 39		11 52		19 43		19 32	
24	10 41		11 50		19 45		19 30	
25	10 43		11 48		19 46		19 28	
26	10 45		11 46		19 47		19 26	
27	10 46		11 44		19 49		19 25	
28	10 48		11 42		19 50		19 23	
29	10 50		11 40		19 52		19 21	
00	10 52		11 38		19 53		19 19	
01	10 54		11 35		19 55		19 17	
02	10 56		11 33		19 56		19 15	
03	10 58		11 31		19 57		19 14	
04	11 00		11 29		19 59		19 12	
05	11 02		11 27		20 00	81	19 10	
06	11 04		11 25		20 02		19 08	
07	11 06		11 23		20 03		19 07	
08	11 08		11 21		20 04		19 05	
09	11 10		11 19		20 06		19 03	
10	11 12		11 17		20 07		19 01	
11	11 14		11 15		20 08		19 00	
12	11 16		11 13		20 10		18 58	
13	11 18		11 10		20 11		18 56	
14	11 20		11 08		20 12		18 54	
15	11 22		11 06		20 14		18 53	
16	11 23		11 04		20 15		18 51	
17	11 25		11 02		20 16		18 50	84
18	11 27		11 00		20 18		18 48	
19	11 29		10 58		20 19		18 46	
20	11 31		10 56		20 20		18 45	
21	11 33		10 54		20 21		18 43	
22	11 35		10 52		20 23		18 42	
23	11 37		10 50		20 24		18 40	
24	11 39		10 48		20 25		18 39	
25	11 41		10 46		20 26		18 37	
26	11 43		10 44		20 27		18 36	
27	11 45		10 42		20 29		18 34	
28	11 47		10 40		20 30		18 33	
29	11 48		10 38		20 31		18 31	
00 ♍	11 50		10 36		20 32		18 30	
01	11 52		10 34		20 33		18 29	
02	11 54		10 32		20 34		18 27	
03	11 56		10 30		20 35		18 26	
04	11 58		10 28		20 36		18 25	
05	11 59		10 26		20 37		18 24	
06	12 01		10 24		20 38		18 22	

☉	☿ NN	V	☿ SN	V	♀ NN	V	♀ SN	V
06 ♍	17 ♌ 52	00	26 ♍27	15	04 ♌ 04	20	15 ♎ 03	16
07	18 52	-01	27 13		04 42		15 45	
08	19 52		28 00	16	05 20		16 27	
09	20 53		28 46		05 59		17 08	
10	21 54	-02	29 32		06 37		17 49	17
11	22 55		00 ♎17		07 16	19	18 30	
12	23 57	-03	01 03		07 54		19 11	
13	24 59		01 48	17	08 33		19 52	
14	26 02	-04	02 34		09 12		20 32	
15	27 05		03 19		09 51		21 12	
16	28 08		04 04		10 30		21 52	18
17	29 11	-05	04 49		11 09		22 32	
18	00 ♍16	-06	05 33		11 49		23 12	
19	01 20		06 18	18	12 28		23 51	
20	02 25	-07	07 03		13 08	18	24 31	
21	03 30		07 47		13 48		25 10	
22	04 36	-08	08 31		14 28		25 49	
23	05 42		09 15		15 08		26 28	19
24	06 49	-09	09 59		15 49		27 07	
25	07 56		10 43		16 30		27 46	
26	09 03	-10	11 27	19	17 10	17	28 24	
27	10 11		12 11		17 51		29 03	
28	11 20	-11	12 55		18 33		29 41	
29	12 29		13 38		19 14		00 ♏19	
00 ♎	13 38	-12	14 21		19 56		00 57	
01	14 48		15 05		20 38	16	01 35	
02	15 58	-13	15 48		21 20		02 13	20
03	17 09	-14	16 31		22 02		02 51	
04	18 21		17 14	20	22 45		03 28	
05	19 32	-15	17 57		23 28		04 06	
06	20 45		18 40		24 11	15	04 43	
07	21 58	-16	19 23		24 55		05 21	
08	23 11	-17	20 06		25 38		05 58	
09	24 25		20 49		26 23	14	06 35	
10	25 39	-18	21 31		27 07		07 12	
11	26 54		22 14		27 52		07 49	
12	28 09	-19	22 56		28 37		08 26	
13	29 25		23 39		29 23	13	09 03	21
14	00 ♎42	-20	24 21	21	00 ♍09		09 40	
15	01 58	-21	25 03		00 55	12	10 16	
16	03 16		25 46		01 42		10 53	
17	04 34	-22	26 28		02 29		11 30	
18	05 52		27 10		03 17	11	12 06	
19	07 11	-23	27 52		04 06		12 42	
20	08 30	-24	28 34		04 54	10	13 19	
21	09 50		29 16		05 44		13 55	
22	11 11	-25	29 58		06 34	09	14 31	
23	12 31		00 ♏40		07 24		15 07	
24	13 53	-26	01 21		08 16	08	15 43	
25	15 14		02 03		09 08	07	16 19	
26	16 37	-27	02 45		10 00		16 55	
27	17 59		03 27		10 54	06	17 31	
28	19 22	-28	04 08	22	11 54	05	18 07	22

☉	♂ NN	V	♂ SN	V	♃ NN	V	♃ SN	V
06 ♍	28 ♊ 29	39	21 ♎ 30	32	18 ♋ 15	54	29 ♐ 43	66
07	28 44		21 51		18 22		29 39	
08	28 58	40	22 11		18 29		29 34	65
09	29 12		22 32		18 35		29 29	
10	29 25		22 53		18 42		29 25	
11	29 38	41	23 15		18 48	55	29 21	
12	29 51		23 36	31	18 55		29 18	64
13	00 ♋ 03		23 57		19 01		29 14	
14	00 15	42	24 19		19 07		29 11	
15	00 26		24 40		19 13		29 08	
16	00 37	43	25 02		19 19		29 05	
17	00 47		25 23		19 24		29 03	63
18	00 57	44	25 45		19 30	56	29 01	
19	01 06		26 07		19 35		28 59	
20	01 15	45	26 29		19 40		28 57	
21	01 23		26 51		19 46		28 55	62
22	01 31	46	27 13		19 51		28 54	
23	01 37	47	27 35	30	19 55		28 53	
24	01 44		27 57		20 00		28 52	
25	01 49	48	28 19		20 05	57	28 51	61
26	01 54		28 42		20 09		28 50	
27	01 58	49	29 04		20 13		28 50	
28	02 01	50	29 26		20 17		28 50	
29	02 04	51	29 49		20 21		28 50	
00 ♎	02 05		00 ♏ 11		20 25		28 51	60
01	02 06	52	00 34		20 29	58	28 51	
02	02 05	53	00 56		20 32		28 52	
03	02 04	54	01 19		20 35		28 53	
04	02 02	55	01 42		20 39		28 54	
05	01 58	56	02 04		20 42		28 55	59
06	01 54	57	02 27		20 44		28 57	
07	01 48	58	02 50		20 47	59	28 58	
08	01 41	59	03 13		20 49		29 00	
09	01 32	60	03 36	29	20 52		29 02	
10	01 22	62	03 59		20 54		29 05	58
11	01 11	63	04 22		20 55		29 07	
12	00 58	64	04 44		20 57	60	29 10	
13	00 43	66	05 08		20 59		29 12	
14	00 27	67	05 31		21 00		29 15	
15	00 09	69	05 54		21 01		29 18	
16	29 ♊ 49	70	06 17		21 02		29 22	57
17	29 27	72	06 40		21 03	61	29 25	
18	29 02	74	07 03		21 03		29 29	
19	28 36	75	07 26		21 04		29 32	
20	28 07	77	07 49		21 04		29 36	
21	27 36	79	08 12		21 04		29 40	
22	27 02	82	08 36		21 03	62	29 45	56
23	26 25	84	08 59		21 03		29 49	
24	25 46	86	09 22		21 02		29 54	
25	25 03	89	09 46		21 01		29 58	
26	24 18	91	10 09		21 00		00 ♑ 03	
27	23 29	94	10 32		20 59	63	00 08	
28	22 36	96	10 55		20 57		00 13	

☉	♄ NN	V	♄ SN	V	♅ NN	V	♅ SN	V
06 ♍	27 ♋ 14	48	19 ♑ 00	56	16 ♊ 42	30	10 ♐ 43	31
07	27 19		18 56		16 43		10 43	30
08	27 24		18 52		16 43		10 43	
09	27 28		18 48		16 44		10 43	
10	27 33		18 44		16 44		10 43	
11	27 37	49	18 40		16 44		10 43	
12	27 42		18 36		16 45		10 43	
13	27 46		18 32		16 45		10 43	
14	27 50		18 29	55	16 45		10 43	
15	27 54		18 25		16 45	31	10 43	
16	27 59		18 22		16 45		10 44	
17	28 03		18 18		16 45		10 44	
18	28 07		18 15		16 45		10 45	
19	28 11		18 12		16 45		10 45	
20	28 14		18 09		16 45		10 46	
21	28 18		18 06		16 44		10 46	
22	28 22		18 04		16 44		10 47	
23	28 26		18 01		16 44		10 47	
24	28 29		17 58		16 43		10 48	
25	28 32		17 56	54	16 43		10 49	
26	28 36	50	17 54		16 42		10 50	
27	28 39		17 52		16 42		10 51	
28	28 42		17 49		16 41		10 52	
29	28 45		17 47		16 40		10 53	
00 ♎	28 48		17 46		16 39		10 54	
01	28 51		17 44		16 39		10 55	
02	28 54		17 42		16 38		10 56	
03	28 57		17 41		16 37		10 57	
04	29 00		17 39		16 36		10 58	
05	29 02		17 38	53	16 35		11 00	
06	29 05		17 37		16 34		11 01	
07	29 07		17 36		16 33		11 02	
08	29 09	51	17 35		16 31		11 04	
09	29 11		17 34		16 30		11 05	
10	29 13		17 33		16 29		11 07	
11	29 15		17 33		16 28		11 08	
12	29 17		17 32		16 26		11 10	
13	29 19		17 32		16 25		11 12	
14	29 21		17 31		16 23		11 13	
15	29 22		17 31	52	16 22		11 15	
16	29 24		17 31		16 20		11 17	
17	29 25		17 31		16 18		11 19	
18	29 26		17 31		16 17		11 20	29
19	29 27	52	17 31		16 15		11 22	
20	29 29		17 32		16 13		11 24	
21	29 29		17 32		16 11	32	11 26	
22	29 30		17 32		16 09		11 28	
23	29 31		17 33		16 07		11 30	
24	29 32		17 34		16 05		11 32	
25	29 32		17 35		16 03		11 34	
26	29 32		17 35		16 01		11 36	
27	29 33		17 36	51	15 59		11 39	
28	29 33		17 38		15 57		11 41	

☉	Ψ NN	V	Ψ SN	V	♀ NN	V	♀ SN	V
06 ♍	12 ♌ 01	64	10 ♒ 24	68	20 ♋ 38	81	18 ♑ 22	84
07	12 03		10 22		20 39		18 21	
08	12 05		10 21		20 40		18 20	
09	12 06		10 19		20 41		18 19	
10	12 08		10 17		20 42		18 18	
11	12 10		10 15		20 43		18 17	
12	12 12		10 14		20 44		18 15	
13	12 13		10 12		20 45		18 14	
14	12 15		10 10		20 46		18 13	
15	12 17		10 08		20 47		18 12	83
16	12 18		10 07		20 47		18 11	
17	12 20		10 05		20 48		18 11	
18	12 21		10 03		20 49		18 10	
19	12 23		10 02		20 50		18 09	
20	12 24		10 00		20 51		18 08	
21	12 26		09 59		20 51		18 07	
22	12 27		09 57		20 52		18 06	
23	12 29		09 56		20 53		18 06	
24	12 30	65	09 54		20 53	82	18 05	
25	12 32		09 53		20 54		18 04	
26	12 33		09 51		20 54		18 04	
27	12 35		09 50		20 55		18 03	
28	12 36		09 49		20 56		18 02	
29	12 37		09 47		20 56		18 02	
00 ♎	12 39		09 46		20 57		18 01	
01	12 40		09 45	67	20 57		18 01	
02	12 41		09 44		20 58		18 00	
03	12 43		09 42		20 58		18 00	
04	12 44		09 41		20 58		17 59	
05	12 45		09 40		20 59		17 59	
06	12 46		09 39		20 59		17 59	
07	12 47		09 38		21 00		17 58	
08	12 48		09 37		21 00		17 58	82
09	12 49		09 36		21 00		17 58	
10	12 50		09 35		21 00		17 57	
11	12 51		09 34		21 01		17 57	
12	12 52		09 33		21 01		17 57	
13	12 53		09 32		21 01		17 57	
14	12 54		09 31		21 01		17 57	
15	12 55		09 30		21 01		17 57	
16	12 56		09 30		21 02		17 57	
17	12 57		09 29		21 02		17 57	
18	12 58		09 28		21 02		17 57	
19	12 59		09 27		21 02		17 57	
20	12 59		09 27		21 02		17 57	
21	13 00		09 26		21 02		17 57	
22	13 01		09 26		21 02		17 57	
23	13 01		09 25		21 02		17 57	
24	13 02		09 24		21 02	83	17 57	
25	13 03		09 24		21 01		17 58	
26	13 03	66	09 24		21 01		17 58	
27	13 04		09 23		21 01		17 58	
28	13 04		09 23	66	21 01		17 59	

☉	☿ NN	V	☿ SN	V	♀ NN	V	♀ SN	V
28 ♎	19 ♎22	-28	04 ♏08	22	11 ♍48	05	18 ♏07	22
29	20 46		04 50		12 43		18 43	
00 ♏	22 09	-29	05 31		13 39	04	19 18	
01	23 34		06 13		14 35	03	19 54	
02	24 58	-30	06 54		15 33	02	20 30	
03	26 23		07 36		16 32	01	21 05	
04	27 48		08 17		17 32	00	21 41	
05	29 14	-31	08 59		18 33	-01	22 16	
06	00 ♏40		09 40		19 35	-02	22 52	
07	02 06		10 21		20 39	-03	23 27	
08	03 33	-32	11 03		21 44	-04	24 03	
09	04 59		11 44		22 50	-06	24 38	
10	06 26		12 25		23 58	-07	25 13	
11	07 53		13 07		25 08	-09	25 48	
12	09 21	-33	13 48		26 19	-10	26 24	
13	10 48		14 29		27 32	-12	26 59	
14	12 16		15 10		28 48	-14	27 34	
15	13 44		15 52		00 ♎05	-16	28 09	
16	15 11		16 33		01 25	-18	28 44	
17	16 39		17 14		02 47	-20	29 19	
18	18 07		17 55		04 11	-23	29 54	
19	19 35		18 36		05 38	-25	00 ♐29	
20	21 03		19 18		07 09	-28	01 04	
21	22 31		19 59		08 42	-31	01 39	
22	23 58		20 40		10 19	-34	02 14	23
23	25 26		21 21		11 59	-37	02 49	
24	26 54		22 02		13 44	-41	03 24	
25	28 21	-32	22 44		15 32	-45	03 59	
26	29 49		23 25		17 24	-49	04 33	
27	01 ♐16		24 06		19 22	-53	05 08	
28	02 43		24 47		21 24	-58	05 48	
29	04 09	-31	25 28		23 31	-63	06 18	
00 ♐	05 36		26 10		25 44	-68	06 52	
01	07 02		26 51		28 03	-73	07 27	
02	08 28	-30	27 32		00 ♏28	-79	08 02	
03	09 54		28 13		02 59	-85	08 36	
04	11 19		28 55		05 31	-91	09 11	
05	12 44	-29	29 36		08 22	-91	09 46	
06	14 08		00 ♐17		11 13	-103	10 20	
07	15 33	-28	00 59		14 12	-109	10 55	
08	16 56		01 40		17 17	-116	11 30	
09	18 20	-27	02 21		20 29	-122	12 04	
10	19 43		03 03		23 48	-128	12 39	
11	21 05	-26	03 44		27 13	-133	13 13	
12	22 28		04 26		00 ♐43	-137	13 48	
13	23 49	-25	05 07		04 18	-147	14 22	
14	25 11		05 49		07 57	-144	14 57	
15	26 31	-24	06 31		11 38	-146	15 32	
16	27 52	-23	07 12		15 21	-141	16 06	
17	29 11		07 54		19 05		16 41	
18	00 ♑31	-22	08 36		22 47	-146	17 15	
19	01 50		09 18		26 28	-144	17 50	
20	03 08	-21	09 59		00 ♑06	-141	18 24	

☉	♂ NN	V	♂ SN	V	♃ NN	V	♃ SN	V
28 ♎	22 ♊ 36	96	10 ♏ 55	29	20 ♋ 57	63	00 ♑ 13	56
29	21 40	99	11 19		20 55		00 18	
00 ♏	20 41	102	11 42		20 53		00 23	55
01	19 37	105	12 05		20 51	64	00 29	
02	18 30	108	12 29		20 49		00 34	
03	17 18	111	12 52		20 46		00 40	
04	16 02	114	13 16		20 43		00 46	
05	14 42	117	13 39		20 40		00 52	
06	13 18	120	14 02	28	20 37	65	00 58	
07	11 49	123	14 26		20 33		01 04	
09	10 16	126	14 49		20 29		01 10	54
09	08 39	129	15 13		20 25		01 17	
10	06 58	132	15 36		20 21	66	01 23	
11	05 13	134	15 59		20 17		01 30	
12	03 24	136	16 23		20 12		01 37	
13	01 32	138	16 46		20 07		01 44	
14	29 ♉ 37	140	17 10		20 02	67	01 50	
15	27 39	141	17 33		19 56		01 57	
16	25 39	142	17 56		19 51		02 05	
17	23 38		18 20		19 45		02 12	53
18	21 36		18 43		19 39		02 19	
19	19 33	141	19 07		19 32	68	02 26	
20	17 30	140	19 30		19 26		02 34	
21	15 27	139	19 53		19 19		02 41	
22	13 27	137	20 17		19 12		02 49	
23	11 27	135	20 40		19 05	69	02 57	
24	09 30	132	21 03		18 57		03 05	
25	07 36	130	21 27		18 49		03 13	
26	05 44	126	21 50		18 41		03 20	
27	03 57	123	22 13		18 33		03 28	
28	02 12	120	22 37		18 25	70	03 37	
29	00 32	116	23 00		18 16		03 45	52
00 ♐	28 ♈ 56	113	23 23		18 07		03 53	
01	27 24	109	23 46		17 58		04 01	
02	25 56	105	24 10		17 49	71	04 10	
03	24 33	102	24 33		17 39		04 18	
04	23 14	99	24 56		17 30		04 27	
05	21 59	95	25 19		17 20		04 35	
06	20 48	92	25 42		17 10		04 44	
07	19 41	89	26 06		16 59	72	04 52	
08	18 39	86	26 29		16 49		05 01	
09	17 40	83	26 52		16 38		05 10	
10	16 44	80	27 15		16 27		05 19	
11	15 52	77	27 38		16 16		05 27	
12	15 04	75	28 01		16 05		05 36	
13	14 19	72	28 24		15 53	73	05 45	
14	13 37	70	28 47		15 42		05 54	
15	12 58	68	29 10		15 30		06 03	
16	12 22	66	29 33		15 18		06 12	
17	11 48	64	29 56		15 06		06 21	51
18	11 17	62	00 ♐ 19		14 53		06 31	
19	10 48	60	00 41		14 41	74	06 40	
20	10 22	58	01 04		14 28		06 49	

☉	♄ NN	V	♄ SN	V	♅ NN	V	♅ SN	V
28 ♎	29 ♋33	52	17 ♑38	51	15 ♊57	32	11 ♐41	29
29	29 33	53	17 39		15 55		11 43	
00 ♏	29 33		17 40		15 53		11 45	
01	29 32		17 41		15 50		11 48	
02	29 32		17 43		15 48		11 50	
03	29 32		17 45		15 46		11 52	
04	29 31		17 46		15 43		11 55	
05	29 30		17 48		15 41		11 57	
06	29 30		17 50		15 38		12 00	
07	29 29		17 52		15 36		12 02	
08	29 28		17 54		15 33		12 05	
09	29 26	54	17 56	50	15 30		12 07	
10	29 25		17 58		15 28		12 10	
11	29 24		18 00		15 25		12 12	
12	29 22		18 03		15 22		12 15	
13	29 21		18 05		15 20		12 17	
14	29 19		18 08		15 17		12 20	
15	29 17		18 10		15 14		12 23	
16	29 15		18 13		15 11		12 25	
17	29 13		18 16		15 08		12 28	
18	29 11		18 19		15 06		12 31	
19	29 08	55	18 21		15 03		12 34	
20	29 06		18 24		15 00		12 36	
21	29 03		18 27		14 57		12 39	
22	29 01		18 31		14 54		12 42	
23	28 58		18 34		14 51		12 45	
24	28 55		18 37	49	14 48		12 47	
25	28 52		18 40		14 45		12 50	
26	28 48		18 44		14 42		12 53	
27	28 45		18 47		14 38		12 56	
28	28 42	56	18 51		14 35		12 59	
29	28 38		18 54		14 32		13 02	
00 ♐	28 35		18 58		14 29		13 05	
01	28 31		19 02		14 26		13 08	
02	28 27		19 06		14 23		13 10	
03	28 23		19 10		14 20		13 13	
04	28 19		19 13		14 16		13 16	
05	28 15		19 17		14 13		13 19	
06	28 10		19 21		14 10		13 22	
07	28 06		19 25		14 07		13 25	
08	28 01		19 30		14 04		13 28	
09	27 57	57	19 34		14 00		13 31	
10	27 52		19 38		13 57		13 34	
11	27 47		19 42		13 54		13 37	
12	27 42		19 47		13 51		13 40	
13	27 37		19 51	48	13 47		13 43	
14	27 32		19 55		13 44		13 46	
15	27 27		20 00		13 41		13 49	
16	27 21		20 04		13 38		13 52	
17	27 16		20 09		13 34		13 55	
18	27 10		20 14		13 31		13 58	
19	27 05		20 18		13 28		14 00	
20	26 59		20 23		13 25		14 03	

☉	Ψ NN		V	Ψ SN		V	♀ NN		V	♀ SN		V
28 ♎	13 ♌	04	66	09 ♒	23	66	21 ♋	01	83	17 ♑	59	82
29	13	05		09	22		21	01		17	59	
00 ♏	13	05		09	22		21	01		17	59	
01	13	06		09	22		21	00		18	00	
02	13	06		09	22		21	00		18	00	81
03	13	06		09	21		21	00		18	01	
04	13	07		09	21		20	59		18	01	
05	13	07		09	21		20	59		18	02	
06	13	07		09	21		20	59		18	02	
07	13	07		09	21		20	58		18	03	
08	13	07		09	21		20	58		18	03	
09	13	08		09	21		20	57		18	04	
10	13	08		09	21		20	57		18	05	
11	13	08		09	21		20	56		18	05	
12	13	08		09	21		20	56		18	06	
13	13	08		09	21		20	55		18	07	
14	13	08		09	21		20	55		18	08	
15	13	08		09	22		20	54		18	08	
16	13	08		09	22		20	53		18	09	
17	13	07		09	22		20	53		18	10	
18	13	07		09	22		20	52		18	11	
19	13	07		09	23		20	51		18	12	
20	13	07		09	23		20	51		18	13	
21	13	07		09	24		20	50		18	14	
22	13	06		09	24		20	49		18	15	
23	13	06	67	09	24		20	48		18	16	
24	13	05		09	25		20	48	84	18	17	
25	13	05		09	25	65	20	47		18	18	
26	13	05		09	26		20	46		18	19	
27	13	04		09	27		20	45		18	20	
28	13	04		09	27		20	44		18	21	
29	13	03		09	28		20	43		18	22	
00 ♐	13	02		09	29		20	42		18	23	
01	13	02		09	29		20	41		18	24	
02	13	01		09	30		20	40		18	26	
03	13	01		09	31		20	39		18	27	
04	13	00		09	32		20	38		18	28	80
05	12	59		09	33		20	37		18	29	
06	12	58		09	33		20	36		18	31	
07	12	57		09	34		20	35		18	32	
08	12	57		09	35		20	34		18	33	
09	12	56		09	36		20	33		18	35	
10	12	55		09	37		20	32		18	36	
11	12	54		09	38		20	31		18	37	
12	12	53		09	39		20	30		18	39	
13	12	52		09	40		20	29		18	40	
14	12	51		09	41		20	27		18	41	
15	12	50		09	42		20	26		18	43	
16	12	49		09	44		20	25		18	44	
17	12	48		09	45		20	24		18	46	
18	12	46		09	46		20	23		18	47	
19	12	45		09	47		20	21		18	49	
20	12	44		09	48		20	20		18	50	

⊙	☿ NN	V	☿ SN	V	♀ NN	V	♀ SN	V
20 ♐	03 ♑ 08	-21	09 ♐ 59	22	00 ♑ 06	-141	18 ♐ 24	23
21	04 26	-20	10 41		03 39	-137	18 59	
22	05 43		11 23		07 08	-132	19 33	
23	07 00	-19	12 05		10 31	-127	20 08	
24	08 16	-18	12 47		13 48	-121	20 42	
25	09 32		13 29		16 59	-115	21 17	
26	10 47	-17	12 12	21	20 02	-108	21 51	
27	12 02		14 54		22 59	-102	22 26	
28	13 16	-16	15 36		25 49	-96	23 01	
29	14 29	-15	16 19		28 31	-89	23 35	
00 ♑	15 43		17 01		01 ♒ 07	-83	24 10	
01	16 55	-14	17 43		03 37	-78	24 44	
02	18 07		18 26		06 00	-72	25 19	
03	19 19	-13	19 09		08 17	-67	25 53	
04	20 30	-12	19 51		10 28	-62	26 28	
05	21 20		19 34		12 34	-57	27 03	
06	22 51	-11	21 17		14 35	-52	27 37	
07	24 00		22 00		16 31	-48	28 12	
08	25 09	-10	22 43		18 22	-44	28 47	
09	26 18	-09	22 26	20	20 09	-40	29 21	
10	27 26		23 10		21 53	-37	29 56	
11	28 34	-08	24 53		23 32	-33	01 ♑ 30	
12	29 41		25 36		25 07	-30	01 05	
13	00 ♒ 48	-07	26 20		26 40	-27	01 40	
14	01 54		27 04		28 09	-25	02 15	
15	03 00	-06	27 47		29 35	-22	02 49	
16	04 05		28 31		00 ♓ 59	-20	03 24	
17	05 10	-05	29 15		02 20	-18	03 59	
18	06 15	-04	00 ♑ 00	19	03 39	-16	04 34	
19	07 19		00 44		04 55	-14	05 09	
20	08 22	-03	01 28		06 10	-12	05 44	
21	09 26		02 13		07 22	-10	06 19	
22	10 29	-02	02 57		08 33	-08	06 54	
23	11 31		03 42		09 42	-07	07 29	
24	12 33		04 27	18	10 49	-06	08 04	22
25	13 35	-01	05 12		11 55	-04	08 39	
26	14 36		05 58		12 59	-03	09 14	
27	15 37	00	06 43		14 02	-02	09 49	
28	16 37		07 28		15 04	-01	10 24	
29	17 37	01	08 14		16 04	01	11 00	
00 ♒	18 37		09 00	17	17 04	02	11 35	
01	19 36		09 46		18 02		12 10	
02	20 36	02	10 32		18 59	03	12 46	
03	21 34		11 19		19 55	04	13 21	
04	22 33	03	12 05		20 51	05	13 56	
05	23 31		12 52	16	21 45		14 32	
06	24 29		13 39		22 39	06	15 07	
07	25 26	04	14 26		23 32	07	15 43	
08	26 23		15 14		24 24	08	16 19	
09	27 20		16 01	15	25 15		16 54	
10	28 16	05	16 49		26 06	09	17 30	
11	29 13		17 37		26 56	10	18 06	
12	00 ♓ 09	06	18 25		27 45		18 42	

☉	♂ NN	V	♂ SN	V	♃ NN	V	♃ SN	V
20 ♐	10 ♈ 22	58	01 ♐ 04	28	14 ♋ 28	74	06 ♑ 49	51
21	09 58	57	01 27		14 16		06 58	
22	09 36	55	01 50		14 03		07 08	
23	09 16	54	02 12		13 50		07 17	
24	08 58	53	02 35		13 37		07 26	
25	08 42	52	02 58		13 24		07 36	
26	08 27	50	03 20		13 10		07 45	
27	08 14	49	03 43		12 57		07 54	
28	08 03	48	04 05		12 43		08 04	
29	07 53	47	04 28		12 30	75	08 13	
00 ♑	07 44	46	04 50		12 16		08 23	
01	07 37	45	05 12		12 02		08 32	
02	07 31		05 35		11 49		08 42	
03	07 26	44	05 57		11 35		08 51	
04	07 22	43	06 19		11 21		09 01	
05	07 19	42	06 41		11 07		09 10	
06	07 18		07 03		10 53		09 20	
07	07 17	41	07 25		10 39		09 29	
08	07 17	40	07 47		10 25		09 39	
09	07 19		08 09		10 11		09 48	
10	07 20	39	08 31		09 56		09 57	
11	07 23		08 53		09 42		10 07	
12	07 27	38	09 15		09 28		10 16	
13	07 31		09 36		09 14		10 26	
14	07 36	37	09 58		09 00		10 35	
15	07 42		10 19		08 46		10 45	
16	07 48		10 41		08 32		10 54	
17	07 55	36	11 02		08 18		11 04	
18	08 03		11 24		08 04		11 13	
19	08 11	35	11 45		07 50	74	11 23	
20	08 20		12 06		07 36		11 32	
21	08 29		12 27		07 23		11 42	
22	08 39	34	12 48		07 09		11 51	
23	08 49		13 09		06 56		12 00	
24	09 00		13 30		06 42		12 10	
25	09 11		13 51		06 29		12 19	
26	09 22	33	14 12		06 16		12 29	
27	09 34		14 32	29	06 03		12 38	
28	09 47		14 53		05 50		12 47	
29	10 00		15 13		05 37	73	12 56	
00 ♒	10 13	32	15 34		05 24		13 06	
01	10 26		15 54		05 12		13 15	
02	10 40		16 14		04 59		13 24	
03	10 54		16 34		04 47		13 33	
04	11 09		16 54		04 35		13 42	
05	11 24		17 14		04 23	72	13 51	
06	11 39	31	17 33		04 11		14 00	
07	11 54		17 53		04 00		14 09	
08	12 10		18 12		03 48		14 18	52
09	12 26		18 31		03 37		14 27	
10	12 42		18 50		03 26		14 36	
11	12 58		19 09		03 15	71	14 45	
12	13 15	30	19 28		03 01		14 54	

☉	♄ NN	V	♄ SN	V	♅ NN	V	♅ SN	V
20 ♐	26 ♋ 59	57	20 ♑ 23	48	13 ♊ 25	32	14 ♐ 03	29
21	26 53	58	20 28		13 22		14 06	
22	26 47		20 32		13 18		14 09	
23	26 41		20 37		13 15		14 12	
24	26 35		20 42		13 12		14 15	
25	26 29		20 47		13 09		14 18	
26	26 23		20 52		13 06		14 21	
27	26 17		20 57		12 03		14 24	
28	26 10		21 02		12 59		14 27	
29	26 04		21 07		12 56		14 29	
00 ♑	25 58		21 12		12 53		14 32	
01	25 51		21 17		12 50		14 35	
02	25 44		21 22		12 47		14 38	
03	25 38		21 27		12 44		14 41	
04	25 31		21 32		12 41		14 44	
05	25 24		21 37		12 38		14 46	
06	25 17		21 42		12 35		14 49	
07	25 10		21 48		12 32		14 52	
08	25 03		21 53		12 29		14 55	
09	24 56	59	21 58		12 26		14 57	
10	24 49		22 03		12 23		15 00	
11	24 42		22 08		12 20		15 02	
12	24 35		22 13		12 18		15 05	
13	24 28		22 19		12 15		15 08	
14	24 20		22 24		12 12		15 10	
15	24 13		22 29		12 09		15 13	
16	24 06		22 35		12 07		15 15	
17	23 59		22 40		12 04		15 18	
18	23 51		22 45		12 01		15 21	
19	23 44		22 51		11 59		15 23	
20	23 37		22 56		11 56		15 25	
21	23 29		23 01		11 54		15 28	
22	23 22		23 07		11 51		15 30	30
23	23 15		23 12		11 49		15 33	
24	23 08		23 17		11 47		15 35	
25	23 00		23 23		11 44		15 37	
26	22 53		23 28		11 42		15 40	
27	22 46		23 33		11 40		15 42	
28	22 38		23 39		11 37		15 44	
29	22 31		23 44		11 35		15 46	
00 ≈	22 24		23 50		11 33		15 49	
01	22 16		23 55		11 31		15 51	
02	22 09		24 00		11 29		15 53	
03	22 02		24 05		11 27		15 55	
04	21 55		24 11		11 25		15 57	
05	21 48		24 16		11 23		15 59	
06	21 41		24 21		11 21		16 01	
07	21 34		24 27		11 19		16 03	
08	21 26		24 32		11 18		16 05	
09	21 19	58	24 37		11 16		16 07	
10	21 13		24 42		11 14		16 08	
11	21 06		24 48		11 13		16 10	
12	20 59		24 53		11 11		16 12	

☉	Ψ NN		V	Ψ SN		V	♀ NN		V	♀ SN		V
20 ♐	12 ♌	44	67	09 ♒	48	65	20 ♋	20	84	18 ♑	50	80
21	12	43		09	50		20	19		18	52	
22	12	42	68	09	51		20	18		18	53	
23	12	40		09	52		20	16		18	55	
24	12	39		09	54		20	15		18	56	
25	12	38		09	55		20	14		18	58	
26	12	36		09	56		20	12		18	59	
27	12	35		09	58		20	11		19	01	
28	12	33		09	59		20	10		19	03	
29	12	32		10	01		20	08		19	04	
00 ♑	12	30		10	02	64	20	07		19	06	
01	12	29		10	04		20	06		19	07	
02	12	27		10	05		20	04		19	09	
03	12	26		10	07		20	03		19	11	
04	12	24		10	08		20	01		19	12	
05	12	23		10	10		20	00		19	14	
06	12	21		10	11		19	58		19	16	
07	12	19		10	13		19	57		19	17	
08	12	18		10	14		19	56		19	19	
09	12	16		10	16		19	54		19	21	
10	12	14		10	17		19	52		19	22	
11	12	12		10	19		19	50		19	23	
12	12	10		10	20		19	49		19	25	
13	12	09		10	22		19	48		19	27	
14	12	07		10	24		19	46		19	28	
15	12	05		10	26		19	45		19	30	
16	12	03		10	27		19	43		19	32	
17	12	01		10	29		19	42		19	33	
18	12	00		10	31		19	40		19	35	
19	11	58		10	33		19	39		19	37	
20	11	56		10	34		19	37		19	39	
21	11	54		10	36		19	36		19	40	
22	11	52		10	38		19	34		19	42	
23	11	50		10	40		19	33		19	44	
24	11	48		10	42		19	31		19	45	
25	11	46		10	43		19	30		19	47	
26	11	44		10	45		19	29		19	49	
27	11	42		10	47		19	27		19	50	
28	11	40		10	49		19	26		19	52	
29	11	38		10	51		19	24		19	54	
00 ♒	11	36		10	53		19	23		19	55	
01	11	34		10	54		19	21		19	57	
02	11	32		10	56		19	20		19	59	
03	11	30		10	58		19	18		20	00	
04	11	28		11	00		19	17		20	02	
05	11	26		11	02		19	16		20	04	
06	11	24		11	04		19	14		20	05	
07	11	22		11	06		19	13		20	07	
08	11	20		11	08		19	11		20	09	
09	11	18		11	10		19	10		20	10	
10	11	16		11	11		19 ♋	09		20	12	
11	11	14		11	13		19	07		20	14	
12	11	12		11	15		19	06		20	15	

☉	☿ NN	V	☿ SN	V	♀ NN	V	♀ SN	V
12 ♒	00 ♓ 09	06	18 ♑ 25	15	27 ♓ 45	10	18 ♑ 42	22
13	01 04		19 14	14	28 34	11	19 18	
14	02 00		20 02		29 23		19 54	
15	02 55	07	20 51		00 ♈ 10	12	20 30	
16	03 50		21 41		00 58		21 06	21
17	04 44		22 30	13	01 45	13	21 42	
18	05 39		23 20		02 31		22 18	
19	06 33	08	24 10		03 17		22 55	
20	07 27		25 00	12	04 02	14	23 31	
21	08 20		25 51		04 48		24 08	
22	09 14	09	26 42	11	05 32		24 44	
23	10 07		27 33		06 17	15	25 21	
24	11 00		28 24		07 01		25 58	
25	11 53		29 16		07 44		26 35	
26	12 45	10	00 ♒ 08	10	08 28	16	27 11	
27	13 37		01 01		09 11		27 48	
28	14 30		01 53	09	09 54		28 26	
29	15 22		02 47		10 36		29 03	20
00 ♓	16 13		03 40		11 18	17	29 40	
01	17 05	11	04 34	08	12 00		00 ♒ 17	
02	17 56		05 28		12 42		00 55	
03	18 47		06 23	07	13 23		01 33	
04	19 38		07 18		14 05	18	02 10	
05	20 29		08 14	06	14 46		02 48	
06	21 20	12	09 09		15 26		03 26	
07	22 10		10 06	05	16 07		04 04	
08	23 01		11 03		16 47		04 42	19
09	23 51		12 00	04	17 27		05 21	
10	24 41		12 58		18 07	19	05 59	
11	25 31	13	13 56	03	18 47		06 38	
12	26 20		14 54	02	19 27		07 17	
13	27 10		15 54		20 06		07 56	
14	27 59		16 53	01	20 45		08 35	
15	28 49		17 54		21 24		09 14	18
16	29 38		18 54	00	22 03		09 53	
17	00 ♈ 27		19 56	-01	22 42	20	10 33	
18	01 16	14	20 58		23 21		11 13	
19	02 05		22 00	-02	24 00		11 52	
20	02 53		23 03	-03	24 38		12 33	
21	03 42		24 07	-04	25 16		13 13	17
22	04 30		25 12		25 54		13 53	
23	05 19		26 17	-05	26 33		14 34	
24	06 07		27 23	-06	27 10		15 15	
25	06 55	15	28 29	-07	27 48		15 56	
26	07 43		29 36	-08	28 26		16 37	16
27	08 31		00 ♓ 44	-09	29 04	21	17 19	
28	09 19		01 53		29 41		18 01	
29	10 06		03 02	-10	00 ♉ 19		18 43	
00 ♈	10 54		04 12	-11	00 56		19 25	15

☉	♂ NN	V	♂ SN	V	♃ NN	V	♃ SN	V
12 ♒	13 ♈ 15	30	19 ♐ 28	29	03 ♋ 04	71	14 ♑ 54	52
13	13 32		19 47		02 54		15 02	
14	13 49		20 05		02 44		15 11	
15	14 06		20 24		02 33		15 19	
16	14 24		20 42	30	02 24	70	15 28	
17	14 42		21 00		02 14		15 36	
18	15 00		21 18		02 04		15 45	
19	15 18		21 36		01 55		15 53	
20	15 36		21 53		01 46	69	16 01	
21	15 55		22 10		01 37		16 10	
22	16 14	29	22 28		01 29		16 18	
23	16 33		22 45		01 20		16 26	
24	16 52		23 01		01 12		16 34	
25	17 11		23 18		01 04	68	16 42	
26	17 30		23 34	31	00 57		16 50	53
27	17 50		23 50		00 49		16 57	
28	18 09		24 06		00 42		17 05	
29	18 29		24 21		00 35	67	17 13	
00 ♓	18 49		24 37		00 28		17 20	
01	19 09		24 52		00 21		17 28	
02	19 30		25 06		00 15		17 35	
03	19 50		25 21	32	00 09	66	17 42	
04	20 10		25 35		00 03		17 50	
05	20 31	28	25 49		29 ♓ 58		17 57	
06	20 52		26 02		29 52		18 04	
07	21 13		26 16		29 47	65	18 11	
08	21 34		26 28		29 42		18 17	54
09	21 55		26 41	33	29 37		18 24	
10	22 16		26 53		29 33		18 31	
11	22 37		27 05		29 29		18 37	
12	22 59		27 16		29 25	64	18 43	
13	23 20		27 27	34	29 21		18 50	
14	23 42		27 37		29 17		18 56	
15	24 03		27 47		29 14		19 02	
16	24 25		27 57		29 11	63	19 08	
17	24 47		28 06	35	29 08		19 14	55
18	25 09		28 15		29 06		19 19	
19	25 31		28 23		29 03		19 25	
20	25 53		28 30	36	29 01		19 30	
21	26 15		28 37		28 59	62	19 36	
22	26 37		28 44	37	28 57		19 41	
23	27 00		28 49		28 56		19 46	
24	27 22		28 54		28 54		19 51	
25	27 45		28 59	38	28 53	61	19 55	56
26	28 07		29 02		28 52		20 00	
27	28 30		29 05	39	28 52		20 05	
28	28 52		29 08		28 51		20 09	
29	29 15		29 09	40	28 51		20 13	
00 ♈	29 38		29 09		28 51	60	20 17	

☉	♄ NN	V	♄ SN	V	♅ NN	V	♅ SN	V
12 ≈	20 ♋59	58	24 ♑53	48	11 ♊11	32	16 ♐12	30
13	20 52		24 58		11 09		16 14	
14	20 45		25 03		11 08		16 15	
15	20 39		25 08		11 06		16 17	
16	20 32		25 13		11 05		16 18	
17	20 25		25 18		11 04		16 20	
18	20 19		25 23		11 02		16 21	
19	20 12		25 28		11 01		16 23	
20	20 06		25 33		11 00		16 24	
21	20 00		25 38		10 59		16 26	
22	19 54		25 43		10 58		16 27	
23	19 48		25 48		10 57		16 28	
24	19 41		25 53		10 56		16 30	
25	19 36		25 58		10 55		16 31	
26	19 30		26 02		10 54		16 32	
27	19 24	57	26 07		10 53		16 33	
28	19 18		26 12		10 53		16 34	
29	19 13		26 17		10 52		16 35	
00 ♓	19 07		26 21		10 51		16 36	
01	19 02		26 26		10 51		16 37	
02	18 56		26 30		10 50		16 38	
03	18 51		26 35		10 50		16 38	
04	18 46		26 39		10 49		16 39	
05	18 41		26 44	49	10 49		16 40	
06	18 36		26 48		10 48		16 40	
07	18 31		26 52		10 48		16 41	
08	18 26		26 56		10 48		16 42	31
09	18 22	56	27 01		10 48		16 42	
10	18 17		27 05		10 48		16 42	
11	18 13		27 09		10 48		16 43	
12	18 08		27 13		10 48		16 43	
13	18 04		27 17		10 48		16 43	
14	18 00		27 21		10 48		16 44	
15	17 56		27 25		10 48		16 44	
16	17 52		27 28		10 48		16 44	
17	17 49		27 32		10 48		16 44	
18	17 45		27 36		10 49		16 44	
19	17 41	55	27 39		10 49		16 44	
20	17 38		27 43		10 49		16 44	
21	17 35		27 46		10 50		16 44	
22	17 32		27 50		10 50		16 44	
23	17 29		27 53		10 51		16 43	
24	17 26		27 56		10 52		16 43	
25	17 23		28 00	50	10 52	30	16 43	
26	17 20		28 03		10 53		16 42	
27	17 18		28 06		10 54		16 42	
28	17 15		28 09		10 55		16 41	
29	17 13	54	28 12		10 56		16 40	
00 ♈	17 11		28 15		10 56		16 40	

☉	Ψ NN	V	Ψ SN	V	♀ NN	V	♀ SN	V
12 ≈	11 ♌ 12	68	11 ≈ 15	64	19 ♋ 06	84	20 ♑ 15	80
13	11 10		11 17		19 05		20 17	
14	11 08		11 19		19 03		20 18	
15	11 06		11 21		19 02		20 20	
16	11 04		11 23		19 01		20 21	
17	11 02		11 25		18 59		20 23	
18	11 00		11 27		18 58		20 25	
19	10 58		11 29		18 57		20 26	81
20	10 56		11 31		18 55		20 28	
21	10 54		11 32		18 54		20 29	
22	10 52		11 34		18 53		20 31	
23	10 50		11 36		18 52		20 32	
24	10 48		11 38		18 51		20 33	
25	10 46		11 40		18 49		20 35	
26	10 44		11 42		18 48		20 36	
27	10 42		11 44		18 47		20 38	
28	10 40		11 45		18 46		20 39	
29	10 38		11 47		18 45		20 40	
00 ♓	10 36		11 49		18 44		20 42	
01	10 34		11 51		18 42		20 43	
02	10 32		11 53		18 41		20 45	
03	10 31		11 55		18 40		20 46	
04	10 29		11 56		18 39		20 47	
05	10 27		11 58		18 38		20 48	
06	10 25		12 00		18 37		20 50	
07	10 23		12 02		18 36		20 51	
08	10 21		12 03		18 35		20 52	
09	10 19		12 05		18 34		20 53	
10	10 18		12 07		18 33		20 54	
11	10 16		12 09		18 32		20 56	
12	10 14		12 10		18 32		20 57	
13	10 12		12 12		18 31		20 58	
14	10 11		12 14		18 30		20 59	
15	10 09		12 15		18 29		21 00	
16	10 07		12 17		18 28		21 01	
17	10 06		12 18		18 27		21 02	
18	10 04		12 20		18 27		21 03	
19	10 02		12 22		18 26		21 04	
20	10 01		12 23		18 25	83	21 05	
21	09 59		12 25		18 24		21 06	
22	09 58		12 26		18 24		21 07	82
23	09 56		12 28		18 23		21 07	
24	09 55		12 29		18 22		21 08	
25	09 53		12 31		18 22		21 09	
26	09 52		12 32	65	18 21		21 10	
27	09 50		12 34		18 21		21 11	
28	09 49		12 35		18 20		21 11	
29	09 48		12 36		18 20		21 12	
00 ♈	09 46		12 38		18 19		21 13	

Table 3, Fraction of Century from 1850

Year	Fraction	Year	Fraction	Year	Fraction
1850	1.00	1900	.50	1950	.00
1851	.99	1901	.49	1951	.01
1852	.98	1902	.48	1952	.02
1853	.97	1903	.47	1953	.03
1854	.96	1904	.46	1954	.04
1855	.95	1905	.45	1955	.05
1856	.94	1906	.44	1956	.06
1857	.93	1907	.43	1957	.07
1858	.92	1908	.42	1958	.08
1859	.91	1909	.41	1959	.09
1860	.90	1910	.40	1960	.10
1861	.89	1911	.39	1961	.11
1862	.88	1912	.38	1962	.12
1863	.87	1913	.37	1963	.13
1864	.86	1914	.36	1964	.14
1865	.85	1915	.35	1965	.15
1866	.84	1916	.34	1966	.16
1867	.83	1917	.33	1967	.17
1868	.82	1918	.32	1968	.18
1869	.81	1919	.31	1969	.19
1870	.80	1920	.30	1970	.20
1871	.79	1921	.29	1971	.21
1872	.78	1922	.28	1972	.22
1873	.77	1923	.27	1973	.23
1874	.76	1924	.26	1974	.24
1875	.75	1925	.25	1975	.25
1876	.74	1926	.24	1976	.26
1877	.73	1927	.23	1977	.27
1878	.72	1928	.22	1978	.28
1879	.71	1929	.21	1979	.29
1880	.70	1930	.20	1980	.30
1881	.69	1931	.19	1981	.31
1882	.68	1932	.18	1982	.32
1883	.67	1933	.17	1983	.33
1884	.66	1934	.16	1984	.34
1885	.65	1935	.15	1985	.35
1886	.64	1936	.14	1986	.36
1887	.63	1937	.13	1987	.37
1888	.62	1938	.12	1988	.38
1889	.61	1939	.11	1989	.39
1890	.60	1940	.10	1990	.40
1891	.59	1941	.09	1991	.41
1892	.58	1942	.08	1992	.42
1893	.57	1943	.07	1993	.43
1894	.56	1944	.06	1994	.44
1895	.55	1945	.05	1995	.45
1896	.54	1946	.04	1996	.46
1897	.53	1947	.03	1997	.47
1898	.52	1948	.02	1998	.48
1899	.51	1949	.01	1999	.49
1900	.50	1950	.00	2000	.50

Node Tables
Asteroids

Geocentric Nodes of the Asteroids for every
even degree of the Sun's longitude.

Positions for 1950, with variations for one century.

☉	☊ NN	V	☊ SN	V	♀ NN	V	♀ SN	V
00 ♈	01 ♊ 39	03	00 ♑ 00	03	17 ♍ 39	40	24 ♓ 44	16
01	01 48		11 04		16 54		24 58	
02	01 57		11 08		16 09		25 13	
03	02 07		11 11		15 25		25 27	
04	02 17		11 15		14 41		25 42	
05	02 27		11 18		13 58		25 57	
06	02 37		11 20		13 16		26 11	
07	02 48		11 22		12 34	39	26 26	
08	02 58		11 24		11 53		26 40	
09	03 09		11 26		11 13		26 55	
10	03 20		11 27		10 34		27 09	
11	03 31		11 28		09 55		27 24	
12	03 43		11 28		09 17		27 38	
13	03 54	02	11 28		08 41	38	27 53	
14	04 06		11 27		08 05		28 07	
15	04 18		11 27		07 30		28 22	
16	04 30		11 25		06 56		28 36	
17	04 42		11 24		06 23	37	28 50	
18	04 54		11 22		05 51		29 04	
19	05 06		11 19		05 20		29 19	
20	05 19		11 16		04 49		29 33	
21	05 32		11 12		04 20	36	29 47	
22	05 45		11 08		03 52		00 ♈ 01	
23	05 58		11 04		03 25		00 15	
24	06 11		10 59		02 59	35	00 29	
25	06 24		10 54		02 34		00 43	
26	06 37		10 48		02 10		01 57	
27	06 51		10 41		01 46	34	01 11	
28	07 04		10 34		01 24		01 25	
29	07 18		10 27		01 03		01 38	
00 ♉	07 32	01	10 18		00 43	33	01 52	
01	07 46		10 10		00 23		02 06	
02	08 00		10 01		00 05		02 19	
03	08 14		09 51		29 ♌ 47		02 33	
04	08 28		09 40		29 31	32	02 46	
05	08 42		09 30		29 15		02 59	
06	08 57		09 18		29 00		03 13	
07	09 11		09 06		28 46	31	03 26	
08	09 26		08 53		28 32		03 39	
09	09 40		08 40		28 20		03 52	
10	09 55		08 26		28 08	30	04 05	
11	10 10		08 11		27 58		04 18	
12	10 25		07 56	02	27 47		04 31	
13	10 40		07 40		27 38	29	04 43	
14	10 55		07 24		27 30		04 56	
15	11 10		07 06		27 22		05 08	
16	11 26		06 49		27 14		05 21	
17	11 41		06 30		27 08	28	05 33	
18	11 56	00	06 11		27 02		05 45	
19	12 12		05 51		26 57		05 57	
20	12 27		05 31		26 53		06 09	
21	12 43		05 10		26 49	27	06 21	
22	12 58		04 48		26 45		06 32	

⊙	✷ NN	V	✷ SN	V	⚷ NN	V	⚷ SN	V
01 ♈	15 ♍12	-42	23 ♓22	-18	21 ♊02	37	05 ♒42	29
01	14 40		23 41		21 06		05 56	
02	14 08	-43	23 59		21 09	36	06 09	
03	13 37		24 17		21 14		06 22	
04	13 06		24 35		21 18		06 35	30
05	12 35	-44	24 54	-19	21 23		06 48	
06	12 05		25 12		21 29	35	07 01	
07	11 35		25 30		21 34		07 13	
08	11 06	-45	25 48		21 40		07 26	
09	10 37		26 07		21 46		07 38	
10	10 09		26 25		21 53		07 50	31
11	09 41		26 43		21 59	34	08 01	
12	09 14		27 01		22 07		08 13	
13	08 47	-46	27 19	-20	22 14		08 24	
14	08 21		27 37		22 22		08 35	
15	07 55		27 55		22 29		08 46	
16	07 30		28 13		22 38	33	08 56	32
17	07 06		28 31		22 46		09 06	
18	06 42		28 49		22 55		09 16	
19	06 19		29 07		23 04		09 26	
20	05 56		29 25	-21	23 13		09 35	
21	05 34		29 43		23 22	32	09 44	33
22	05 13		00 ♈01		23 32		09 53	
23	04 52		00 19		23 42		10 01	
24	04 32		00 36		23 52		10 09	
25	04 13		00 54		24 02		10 17	
26	03 54		01 12		24 13		10 25	34
27	03 36		01 29	-22	24 23		10 32	
28	03 19		01 47		24 34	31	10 38	
29	03 02	-45	02 04		24 45		10 45	
00 ♉	02 45		02 21		24 56		10 51	35
01	02 30		02 39		25 08		10 56	
02	02 15		02 56		25 20		11 01	
03	02 01		03 13	-23	25 31		11 06	36
04	01 47		03 30		25 43	30	11 11	
05	01 34		03 47		25 56		11 14	
06	01 21	-44	04 04		26 08		11 18	37
07	01 10		04 21		26 20		11 21	
08	00 58		04 38		26 33		11 23	
09	00 48		04 55	-24	26 46		11 25	38
10	00 38		05 12		26 59		11 27	
11	00 28	-43	05 28		27 12		11 28	
12	00 19		05 45		27 25	29	11 28	
13	00 11		06 01		27 39		11 28	39
14	00 03		06 18		27 52		11 27	
15	29 ♌56	-42	06 34	-25	28 06		11 26	40
16	29 49		06 50		28 20		11 24	
17	29 43		07 06		28 33		11 22	
18	29 37		07 22		28 48		11 19	41
19	29 32	-41	07 38		29 02		11 15	
20	29 27		07 53	-26	29 16		11 11	42
21	29 23		08 09		29 30	28	11 05	
22	29 19		08 24		29 45		11 00	

☉	⚳ NN		V	⚳ SN		V	⚴ NN		V	⚴ SN		V
22 ♉	12 ♊	58	00	04 ♑	48	02	26 ♌	45	27	06 ♈	32	16
23	13	14		04	26		26	43		06	44	
24	13	30		04	03	01	26	41		06	55	
25	14	45		03	39		26	39	26	07	07	
26	14	01		03	15		26	38		07	18	
27	14	17		02	50		26	38		07	29	
28	14	33		02	25		26	38		07	40	
29	14	49		01	59		26	38	25	07	51	
00 ♊	15	05		01	32		26	40		08	01	
01	15	21		01	05		26	41		08	12	
02	15	37		00	37	00	26	43		08	22	17
03	15	53		00	09		26	46	24	08	32	
04	16	10		29 ♐	40		26	49		08	42	
05	16	26	-01	29	11		26	52		08	52	
06	16	42		28	41		26	56		09	02	
07	16	58		28	11		27	00		09	11	
08	17	15		27	40	-01	27	05	23	09	21	
09	17	31		27	09		27	10		09	30	
10	17	47		26	37		27	16		09	39	
11	18	04		26	06		27	21		09	47	
12	18	20		25	33		27	28		09	56	
13	18	36		25	01		27	34		10	04	
14	18	53		24	28	-02	27	41	22	10	12	
15	19	09		23	55		27	48		10	20	
16	19	26		23	22		27	56		10	28	
17	19	42		22	49		28	04		10	36	
18	19	59		22	15		28	12		10	43	
19	20	15		21	41	-03	28	21		10	50	
20	20	31		21	08		28	30	21	10	57	
21	20	48		20	34		28	39		11	03	18
22	21	04		20	00		28	48		11	10	
23	21	21		19	27		28	58		11	16	
24	21	37	-02	18	53	-04	29	08		11	22	
25	21	54		18	20		29	18		11	27	
26	22	10		17	46		29	29		11	33	
27	22	27		17	13		29	39	20	11	38	
28	22	43		16	40		29	50		11	43	
29	23	00		16	07	-05	00 ♍	02		11	47	
00 ♋	23	16		15	35		00	13		11	51	
01	23	33		15	02		00	25		11	55	
02	23	49		14	31		00	37		11	59	
03	24	05		13	59		00	49		12	02	19
04	24	22		13	28		01	01		12	05	
05	24	38		12	57	-06	01	14	19	12	08	
06	24	54		12	27		01	26		12	10	
07	25	11		11	57		01	39		12	12	
08	25	27		11	28		01	52		12	14	
09	25	43		10	59		02	06		12	15	
10	25	59		10	31		02	19		12	16	
11	26	16		10	03	-07	02	33		12	17	20
12	26	32		09	36		02	46		12	17	
13	26	48	-03	09	09		03	00		12	17	
14	27	04		08	43		03	15		12	17	

☉	✴ NN	V	✴ SN	V	✹ NN	V	✹ SN	V
22 ♉	29 ♌ 19	-41	08 ♈ 24	-26	29 ♊ 45	28	11 ♒ 00	42
23	29 16	-40	08 40		00 ♋ 00		10 53	43
24	29 13		08 55		00 14		10 46	
25	29 11		09 10		00 29		10 38	44
26	29 09	-39	09 25	-27	00 44		10 29	
27	29 08		09 40		00 59		10 19	45
28	29 07		09 55		01 14		10 09	
29	29 06		10 09		01 29		09 57	46
00 ♊	29 06		10 24		01 45		09 45	
01	29 07	-38	10 38	-28	02 00	27	09 32	47
02	29 07		10 52		02 16		09 18	48
03	29 08		11 06		02 31		09 03	
04	29 10		11 20		02 47		08 47	49
05	29 12	-37	11 33	-29	02 03		08 30	
06	29 14		11 47		03 18		08 12	50
07	29 17		12 00		03 34		07 53	51
08	29 19		12 13		03 50		07 33	
09	29 23	-36	12 26		04 06		07 12	52
10	29 26		12 39	-30	04 22		06 50	
11	29 30		12 51		04 38		06 27	53
12	29 35		13 04		04 55		06 03	54
13	29 39	-35	13 16		05 11		05 37	
14	29 44		13 28	-31	05 27	26	05 10	55
15	29 50		13 39		05 44		04 43	56
16	29 55		13 51		06 00		04 14	
17	00 ♍ 01	-34	14 02		06 17		03 44	57
18	00 07		14 13		06 33		03 12	58
19	00 13		14 24	-32	06 50		02 40	
20	00 20		14 34		07 06		02 06	59
21	00 27	-33	14 44		07 23		01 32	
22	00 34		14 54		07 40		00 56	60
23	00 42		15 04	-33	07 57		00 18	61
24	00 50		15 13		08 13		29 ♑ 40	
25	00 57	-32	15 22		08 30		29 01	62
26	01 06		15 31	-34	08 47		28 20	
27	01 14		15 40		09 04		27 38	63
28	01 23		15 48		09 21		26 56	
29	01 32		15 56		09 38		26 12	64
00 ♋	01 41	-31	16 03	-35	09 55		25 27	
01	01 50		16 10		10 12		24 41	65
02	02 00		16 17		10 29	25	23 55	
03	02 09		16 24		10 46		23 07	
04	02 19		16 30	-36	11 03		22 19	66
05	02 30	-30	16 36		11 20		21 30	
06	02 40		16 41		11 37		20 40	
07	02 50		16 46	-37	11 54		19 49	
08	03 01		16 50		12 11		18 58	
09	03 12	-29	16 55		12 29		18 07	
10	03 23		16 58	-38	12 46		17 15	
11	03 34		17 01		13 03		16 23	
12	03 46		17 04		13 20		15 31	
13	03 57		17 07	-39	13 37		14 38	
14	04 09	-28	17 08		13 54		13 45	

⊙	⚳ NN	V	⚳ SN	V	⚴ NN	V	⚴ SN	V
14 ♋	27 ♊ 04	-03	08 ♐ 43	-07	03 ♍ 15	19	12 ♈ 17	20
15	27 20		08 17		03 29	18	12 16	
16	27 36		07 52		03 43		12 15	
17	27 52		07 28		03 58		12 13	
18	28 08		07 05		04 13		12 11	21
19	28 23		06 42		04 27		12 09	
20	28 39		06 19	-08	04 42		12 06	
21	28 55		05 58		04 58		12 02	
22	29 11		05 37		05 13		11 59	
23	29 26		05 16		05 28		11 55	
24	29 42		04 56		05 44		11 50	
25	29 57		04 37		05 59		11 45	22
26	00 ♋ 13		04 19		06 15		11 39	
27	00 28		04 01		06 31		11 33	
28	00 43		03 44		06 47	17	11 27	
29	00 59		03 28		07 03		11 20	
00 ♌	01 14		03 12		07 19		11 13	23
01	01 29		02 56		07 36		11 05	
02	01 44		02 42		07 52		10 56	
03	01 59	-04	02 28		08 08		10 47	
04	02 14		02 15		08 25		10 38	
05	02 28		02 02		08 42		10 28	24
06	02 43		01 50		08 58		10 18	
07	02 57		01 39		09 15		10 07	
08	03 12		01 28		09 32		09 55	
09	03 26		01 18		09 49		09 43	
10	03 41		01 08		10 06		09 30	25
11	03 55		00 59		10 23		09 17	
12	04 09		00 50		10 40		09 04	
13	04 23		00 42		10 58		08 50	
14	04 37		00 35		14 15	16	08 35	
15	04 50		00 28		11 32		08 20	26
16	05 04		00 22		11 50		08 04	
17	05 17		00 16		11 07		07 47	
18	05 31		00 11		12 25		07 30	
19	05 44		00 06		12 43		07 13	27
20	05 57		00 02		12 00		06 55	
21	06 10		29 ♏ 58		13 18		06 37	
22	06 23		29 54		13 36		06 17	
23	06 36	-5	29 52		13 54		05 58	28
24	06 48		29 49		13 12		05 38	
25	07 01		29 47		14 29		05 17	
26	07 13		29 46		14 47		04 56	
27	07 25		29 45		14 05		04 34	
28	07 37		29 44		15 23		04 12	29
29	07 49		29 44		15 42		03 50	
00 ♍	08 00		29 44		15 00		03 26	
01	08 12		29 45		16 18		03 03	
02	08 23		29 46		16 36		02 39	30
03	08 34		29 47		16 54		02 14	
04	08 45		29 49		16 12		01 50	
05	08 56		29 51	-07	17 31		01 24	
06	09 06		29 53		17 49		00 59	

⊙	⚹ NN	V	⚹ SN	V	⚹ NN	V	⚹ SN	V
14 ♋	04 ♍09	-28	17 ♈08	-39	13 ♋54	25	13 ♑45	66
15	04 21		17 10		14 12		12 53	
16	04 33		17 11	-40	14 29		12 00	65
17	04 45		17 11		14 46		11 08	
18	04 57		17 11		15 03		10 16	
19	05 10	-27	17 10	-41	15 20		09 24	64
20	05 22		17 09		15 37		08 33	
21	05 35		17 07		15 55		07 42	63
22	05 48		17 04	-42	16 12		06 52	
23	06 01		17 01		16 29		06 02	62
24	06 14	-26	16 57		16 46		05 13	61
25	06 27		16 53	-43	17 03		04 25	
26	06 40		16 48		17 20		03 38	60
27	06 54		16 42		17 37		02 52	59
28	07 07		16 36	-44	17 54		02 06	
29	07 21		16 29		18 11		01 22	58
00 ♌	07 35	-25	16 21		18 28		00 38	57
01	07 48		16 12	-45	18 45		29 ♐56	56
02	08 02		16 03		19 02		29 14	
03	08 16		15 53		19 19		28 34	55
04	08 31		15 42	-46	19 35		27 55	54
05	08 45	-24	15 30		19 52		27 17	53
06	08 59		15 18		20 09		26 40	52
07	09 13		15 04	-47	20 26		26 05	
08	09 28		14 50		20 42		25 30	51
09	09 43		14 35		20 59		24 57	50
10	09 57		14 19	-48	21 15		24 25	49
11	10 12	-23	14 02		21 32		23 54	48
12	10 27		13 44		21 48		23 24	
13	10 41		13 25	-49	22 05		22 55	47
14	10 56		13 06		22 21		22 28	46
15	11 11		12 45		22 38		22 02	
16	11 26		12 23	-50	22 54		21 37	45
17	11 41	-22	12 00		23 10		21 13	44
18	11 57		11 36		23 26		20 50	43
19	12 12		11 12		23 42		20 28	
20	12 27		10 46	-51	23 58		20 07	42
21	12 42		10 19		24 14		19 48	41
22	12 58		09 51		24 30		19 29	
23	13 13	-21	09 22		24 46		19 11	40
24	13 29		08 52		25 01		18 55	
25	13 44		08 21		25 17		18 39	39
26	14 00		07 49		25 33		18 24	
27	14 15		07 16		25 48		18 11	38
28	14 31		06 42		26 03		17 58	
29	14 47		06 07		26 19		17 46	37
00 ♍	15 02	-20	05 31		26 34		17 35	
01	15 18		04 53		26 49		17 24	36
02	15 34		04 15		27 04		17 15	
03	15 49		03 36		27 19		17 06	35
04	16 05		02 56		27 34		16 58	
05	16 21		02 16		27 48		16 51	34
06	16 37	-19	01 34		28 03		16 45	

☉	⚳ NN	V	⚳ SN	V	⚴ NN	V	⚴ SN	V
06 ♍	09 ♋ 06	-05	29 ♏ 53	-07	17 ♍ 49	16	00 ♈ 59	30
07	09 17		29 56		18 07		00 33	31
08	09 27		29 59		18 25		00 06	
09	09 37		00 ♐ 03		18 44		29 ♓ 39	
10	09 47		00 07		19 02		29 12	
11	09 56		00 11		19 20	15	28 45	
12	10 06	-06	00 15		19 39		28 17	
13	10 15		00 20		19 57		27 50	32
14	10 24		00 25		20 16		27 21	
15	10 32		00 30		20 34		26 53	
16	10 41		00 36		20 52		26 25	
17	10 49		00 42		21 11		26 56	
18	10 57		00 48		21 29		25 27	
19	11 04		00 55		21 47		24 58	
20	11 12		01 02		22 06		24 29	
21	11 19		01 09		22 24		24 00	
22	11 26		01 16		22 43		23 31	33
23	11 32		01 23	-06	23 01		23 02	
24	11 39		01 31		23 19		22 33	
25	11 45		01 39		23 38		22 04	
26	11 51		01 47		23 56		21 35	
27	11 56		01 56		24 15		21 07	
28	12 01		02 04		24 33		20 38	
29	12 06		02 13		24 51		20 09	
00 ♎	12 10		02 22		25 09		19 41	
01	12 15	-07	02 31		25 28		19 13	
02	12 18		02 41		26 46		18 45	
03	12 22		02 50		26 04		18 17	
04	12 25		03 00		26 22		17 50	
05	12 28		03 10		26 41		17 23	
06	12 30		03 21		26 59		16 56	32
07	12 32		03 31		27 17		16 29	
08	12 34		03 41		27 35		16 03	
09	12 35		03 52		27 53		15 37	
10	12 36		04 03	-05	28 11		15 12	
11	12 37		04 14		28 29		14 47	
12	12 37		04 25		28 47		14 22	
13	12 36		04 37		29 05		13 58	
14	12 35		04 48		29 23		13 34	
15	12 34		05 00		29 41		13 11	
16	12 33		05 11		29 59		12 48	31
17	12 30		05 23		00 ♎ 17		12 26	
18	12 28		05 35		00 34		12 04	
19	12 25		05 48		00 52		11 43	
20	12 21		06 00		01 10		11 22	
21	12 17		06 12		01 27		11 02	
22	12 13	-08	06 25		01 45		10 42	30
23	12 08		06 37		02 02		10 23	
24	12 02		06 50		02 20		10 04	
25	11 56		07 03		02 37		09 45	
26	11 49		07 16	-04	02 54		09 28	
27	11 42		07 29		03 12		09 10	
28	11 34		07 42		03 29		08 54	29

☉	⚹ NN	V	⚹ SN	V	✩ NN	V	✩ SN	V
06 ♍	16 ♍ 37	-19	01 ♈ 34	-51	28 ♋ 03	25	16 ♐ 45	34
07	16 53		00 51	-50	28 17		16 39	33
08	17 09		00 08		28 32		16 34	
09	17 25		29 ♓ 24		28 46		16 30	
10	17 40		28 40	-49	29 00		16 26	32
11	17 56		27 54		29 14		16 24	
12	18 12		27 09	-48	29 28		16 21	
13	18 28	-18	26 22		29 42	26	16 20	31
14	18 44		25 35	-47	29 55		16 18	
15	19 00		24 48		00 ♌ 09		16 18	
16	19 16		24 01	-46	00 22		16 18	30
17	19 32		23 13	-45	00 35		16 18	
18	19 48		22 25		00 48		16 20	
19	20 04		21 37	-44	01 01		16 21	
20	20 20	-17	20 49	-43	01 14		16 23	29
21	20 36		20 01	-42	01 26		16 26	
22	20 52		19 13		01 39		16 29	
23	21 08		18 25	-41	01 51		16 33	
24	21 24		17 37	-40	02 03		16 37	28
25	21 39		16 50	-39	02 15		16 41	
26	21 55		16 03	-38	02 27		16 46	
27	22 11		15 16	-37	02 39		16 51	
28	22 27	-16	14 30	-36	02 50	27	16 57	
29	22 43		13 44	-35	03 01		17 03	
00 ♎	22 59		12 59		03 12		17 09	27
01	23 15		12 15	-34	03 23		17 16	
02	23 30		11 32	-33	03 34		17 23	
03	23 46		10 49	-32	03 44		17 31	
04	24 02		10 06	-31	03 54		17 39	
05	24 17	-15	09 25	-30	04 04		17 47	
06	24 33		08 45	-29	04 14		17 55	26
07	24 49		08 05	-28	04 24		18 04	
08	25 04		07 26	-27	04 33		18 13	
09	25 20		06 49		04 42	28	18 23	
10	25 35		06 12	-26	04 51		18 32	
11	25 51		05 36	-25	04 59		18 42	
12	26 06		05 01	-24	05 08		18 52	
13	26 22	-14	04 28	-23	05 16		19 03	
14	26 37		03 55		05 24		19 14	25
15	26 52		03 23	-22	05 31		19 25	
16	27 07		02 52	-21	05 39		19 36	
17	27 23		02 23		05 46	29	19 47	
18	27 38		01 54	-20	05 52		19 59	
19	27 53		01 26	-19	05 59		20 11	
20	28 08		01 00		05 05		20 23	
21	28 23	-13	00 34	-18	06 11		20 35	
22	28 38		00 10		06 16		20 48	
23	28 53		29 - 46	-17	06 21	30	21 01	
24	29 07		29 24	-16	06 26		21 14	
25	29 22		29 02		06 31		21 27	
26	29 37		28 41		06 35		21 40	24
27	29 51		28 22	-15	06 38		21 54	
28	00 ♎ 06		28 03		06 42		22 07	

⊙	♃ NN	V	♃ SN	V	♀ NN	V	♀ SN	V
28 ♎	11 ♋34	-08	07 ♐42	-04	03 ♎29	15	08 ♓54	29
29	11 26		07 56		03 46		08 38	
00 ♏	11 17		08 09		04 03		08 22	
01	11 08		08 23		04 20		08 07	
02	10 58		08 36		04 37		07 52	
03	10 47		08 50		04 54		07 38	
04	10 36		09 03		05 11		07 25	28
05	10 24		09 17		05 27		07 12	
06	10 12		09 31		05 44		06 59	
07	09 59		09 45		06 00		06 47	
08	09 45		09 59		06 17		06 36	
09	09 31		10 13		06 33		06 25	
10	09 16		10 28		06 49		06 15	27
11	09 00		10 42		07 06		06 05	
12	08 44		10 56		07 22		05 55	
13	08 27		11 11	-03	07 38		05 46	
14	08 09		11 25		07 54		05 38	
15	07 51		11 40		08 09		05 30	
16	07 32		11 54		08 25		05 23	26
17	07 12		12 09		08 41		05 15	
18	06 52		12 24		08 56		05 09	
19	06 31		12 38		09 12		05 03	
20	06 09		12 53		09 27		04 57	
21	05 47		13 08		09 42		04 52	
22	05 24		13 23		09 57		04 47	25
23	05 01	-07	13 38		10 12		04 43	
24	04 36		13 53		10 27		04 39	
25	04 12		14 08		10 41		04 35	
26	03 46		14 23		10 56		04 32	
27	03 20		14 38		11 10		04 29	
28	02 53		14 53		11 25		04 27	24
29	02 26		15 08		11 39		04 25	
00 ♐	01 58		15 24		11 53		04 24	
01	01 29		15 39		12 06		04 22	
02	01 00		15 54	-02	12 20		04 22	
03	00 31	-06	16 09		12 34		04 21	
04	00 00		16 25		12 47		04 21	
05	29 ♓30		16 40		13 00	16	04 21	
06	28 59		16 56		13 13		04 22	23
07	28 27		17 11		13 26		04 23	
08	27 55		17 26		13 39		04 24	
09	27 23		17 42		13 51		04 26	
10	26 50	-05	17 57		14 03		04 28	
11	26 17		18 13		14 16		04 30	
12	25 44		18 28		14 27		04 32	
13	25 10		18 44		14 39		04 35	
14	24 36		18 59		14 51		04 38	22
15	24 02	-04	19 15		15 02		04 42	
16	23 27		19 30		15 13		04 45	
17	22 53		19 46		15 24		04 49	
18	22 18		20 01		15 35		04 54	
19	21 43		20 17		15 45		04 58	
20	21 09	-03	20 32		15 55		05 03	

☉	⚷ NN	V	⚷ SN	V	⯓ NN	V	⯓ SN	V
28 ♎	00 ♎06	-13	28 ♒03	-15	06 ♌42	30	22 ♐07	24
29	00 20	-12	27 45	-14	06 45	31	22 21	
00 ♏	00 34		27 28		06 48		22 35	
01	00 49		27 12	-13	06 50		22 49	
02	01 03		26 57		06 52		23 03	
03	01 17		26 43		06 53		23 18	
04	01 31		26 29	-12	06 54	32	23 32	
05	01 45		26 17		06 55		23 47	
06	01 59		26 05		06 55		24 02	
07	02 12		25 54		06 55		24 17	
08	02 26	-11	25 44	-11	06 55	33	24 32	
09	02 40		25 34		06 53		24 48	
10	02 53		25 25	-12	06 52		25 03	
11	03 06		25 17		06 50		25 18	
12	03 20		25 10	-10	06 47	34	25 34	
13	03 33		25 03		06 44		25 50	
14	03 46		24 57		06 41		26 06	
15	03 59		24 52		06 37		26 22	
16	04 11		24 47		06 32	35	26 38	
17	04 24		24 43		06 27		26 54	
18	04 37	-10	24 40	-09	06 21		27 10	
19	04 49		24 37		06 15	36	27 27	
20	05 01		24 35		06 08		27 43	
21	05 13		24 33		06 01		28 00	
22	05 25		24 32		05 53	37	28 16	
23	05 37		24 31		05 44		28 33	
24	05 49		24 31		05 35		28 50	
25	06 01		24 31		05 25	38	29 07	
26	06 12		24 32		05 15		29 24	
27	06 24		24 33		05 04		29 41	
28	06 35		24 35	-08	04 52	39	29 58	
29	06 46		24 37		04 39		00 ♑15	
00 ♐	06 57	-09	24 40		04 26	40	00 32	
01	07 07		24 43		04 13		00 50	
02	07 18		24 47		03 58		01 07	
03	07 28		24 51		03 43	41	01 25	
04	07 38		24 55		03 27		01 42	
05	07 48		25 00		03 11	42	02 00	
06	07 58		25 05		02 53		02 17	
07	08 08		25 10		02 35	43	02 35	
08	08 17		25 16		02 17		02 53	
09	08 26		25 22		01 57		03 11	
10	08 35		25 29		01 37	44	03 29	
11	08 44		25 36		01 16		03 46	
12	08 53		25 43		00 54	45	04 04	
13	09 01		25 50		00 32		04 22	
14	09 09		25 58		00 08	46	04 40	
15	09 17		26 06		29 ♋45		04 59	
16	09 25	-08	26 14		29 20	47	05 17	
17	09 33		26 23		28 54		05 35	
18	09 40		26 32		28 28	48	05 53	
19	09 47		26 41		28 01		06 11	
20	09 54		26 51		27 34	49	06 30	

☉	♃ NN	V	♃ SN	V	♀ NN	V	♀ SN	V
20 ♐	21 ♊ 09	-03	20 ♐ 32	-02	15 ♎ 55	16	05 ♓ 03	22
21	20 34		20 48		16 05		05 08	
22	19 59		21 03	-01	16 15		05 13	
23	19 24		21 19		16 25		05 19	21
24	18 50	-02	21 34		16 34		05 25	
25	18 15		21 50		16 43		05 30	
26	17 41		22 05		16 51		05 37	
27	17 07		22 21		17 00	17	05 43	
28	16 33		22 36		17 08		05 50	
29	15 59	-01	22 52		17 16		05 57	
00 ♑	15 26		23 07		17 23		06 04	
01	14 53		23 22		17 30		06 11	
02	14 20		23 38		17 37		06 19	
03	13 48		23 53		17 44		06 26	
04	13 16	00	24 09		17 50		06 34	20
05	12 44		24 24		17 56		06 42	
06	12 13		24 39		18 02		06 51	
07	11 43	01	24 54		18 07		06 59	
08	11 13		25 10		18 12		07 08	
09	10 43		25 25		18 16	18	07 17	
10	11 14		25 40	00	18 20		07 25	
11	09 46		25 55		18 24		07 35	
12	09 18	02	26 10		18 27		07 44	
13	08 51		26 26		18 30		07 54	
14	08 24		26 41		18 32		08 03	
15	07 58		26 56		18 34		08 23	
16	07 32		27 11		18 36		08 21	
17	07 08		27 26		18 37		08 33	
18	06 43	03	27 40		18 37	19	08 43	19
19	06 20		27 55		18 38		08 54	
20	05 57		28 10		18 37		09 04	
21	05 35		28 25		18 36		09 15	
22	05 13		28 40		18 35		09 26	
23	04 52		28 54		18 33		09 37	
24	04 32		29 09		18 30		09 48	
25	04 13		29 23		18 27	20	09 59	
26	03 54	04	29 38		18 24		10 10	
27	03 36		29 52		18 19		10 22	
28	03 18		00 ♑ 06		18 15		10 33	
29	03 01		00 21		18 09		10 45	
00 ♒	02 45		00 35		18 03	21	10 57	
01	02 29		00 49		17 56		11 08	
02	02 14		01 03	01	17 49		11 20	
03	02 00		01 17		17 41		11 33	18
04	01 46		01 31		17 32		11 45	
05	01 33		01 45		17 23	22	11 57	
06	01 21		01 59		17 12		12 09	
07	01 09		02 12		17 01		12 22	
08	00 57		02 26		16 50		12 34	
09	00 47		02 40		16 37	23	12 47	
10	00 37		02 53		16 24		13 00	
11	00 27		03 06		16 10		13 13	
12	00 18		03 19		15 55	24	13 26	

☉	✳NN	V	✳SN	V	✵NN	V	✵SN	V
20 ♐	09 ♎54	-08	26 ♒51	-08	27 ♋34	49	06 ♑30	24
21	10 00		27 00		27 05		06 48	
22	10 07		27 10		26 37	50	07 06	
23	10 13		27 21		26 07		07 25	
24	10 19		27 31		25 36	51	07 43	
25	10 24		27 42	-09	25 06		08 01	
26	10 29		27 53		24 34	52	08 20	
27	10 34		28 04		24 02		08 38	
28	10 39		28 15		23 29		08 57	
29	10 43		28 27		22 55	53	09 15	
00 ♑	10 47		28 38		22 22		09 34	
01	10 51		28 50		21 47	54	09 52	
02	10 54		29 02		21 12		10 11	
03	10 57		29 15		20 37		10 30	
04	11 00		29 27		20 01	55	10 48	
05	11 03		29 40		19 25		11 07	
06	11 05		29 53		18 48		11 25	
07	11 06		00 ♓06		18 11	56	11 44	
08	11 08		00 19		17 34		12 03	
09	11 09		00 32		16 57		12 21	
10	11 10	-9	00 46	-10	16 19	57	12 40	
11	11 10		00 59		15 41		12 59	
12	11 10		01 13		15 03		13 17	
13	11 09		01 27		14 25		13 36	
14	11 08		01 41		13 47	58	13 55	
15	11 07		01 55		13 09		14 13	
16	11 05		02 10		12 31		14 32	
17	11 03		02 24		11 53		14 51	
18	11 00	-10	02 39		11 16		15 09	
19	10 57		02 54		10 38		15 28	
20	10 54		03 09		10 01		15 47	
21	10 50		03 24	-11	09 24		16 05	
22	10 45		03 39		08 47		16 24	
23	10 40		03 54		08 10		16 42	25
24	10 35		04 09		07 34		17 01	
25	10 29	-11	04 25		06 58		17 20	
26	10 22		04 40		06 23	57	17 38	
27	10 16		04 56		05 48		17 57	
28	10 08		05 12		05 14		18 15	
29	10 00		05 28		04 40		18 34	
00 ♒	09 52	-12	05 44		04 07		18 52	
01	09 43		06 00		03 34		19 11	
02	09 33	-13	06 16		03 02	56	19 29	
03	09 23		06 32	-12	02 30		19 48	
04	09 12	-13	06 48		01 58		20 06	
05	09 01		07 05		01 29	55	20 25	
06	08 49		07 21		01 00		20 43	
07	08 36	-14	07 38		00 31		21 01	
08	08 23		07 54		00 03		21 20	
09	08 10		08 11		29 ♓35	54	21 38	
10	07 55	-15	08 28		29 09		21 56	
11	07 41		08 45		28 43	53	22 15	
12	07 25		09 02		28 17		22 33	

☉	☊ NN	V	☊ SN	V	♀ NN	V	♀ SN	V
12 ≈	00 ♊ 18	04	03 ♑ 19	01	15 ♎ 55	24	13 ♓ 26	18
13	00 10		03 33		15 39		13 39	
14	00 02		03 46		15 22		13 52	
15	29 ♉ 55		03 59		15 05	25	14 05	
16	29 48		04 11		14 46		14 18	
17	29 42		04 24		14 27		14 31	
18	29 36		04 37		14 07	26	14 45	
19	29 31	05	04 49		13 46		14 58	
20	29 26	04	05 02		13 24		15 11	
21	29 22		05 14		13 01	27	15 25	
22	29 19		05 26		12 37		15 39	
23	29 15		05 38		12 12		15 52	
24	29 13		05 50		11 46	28	16 06	
25	29 10		06 02		11 19		16 20	17
26	29 09		06 13		10 51	29	16 34	
27	29 07		06 25		10 22		16 47	
28	29 06		06 36		09 52		17 01	
29	29 06		06 47	02	09 22	30	17 15	
00 ♓	29 06		06 58		08 50		17 29	
01	29 06		07 09		08 17	31	17 43	
02	29 07		07 20		07 43		17 58	
03	29 08		07 31		07 09	32	18 12	
04	29 09		07 41		06 33		18 26	
05	29 11		07 51		05 57		18 40	
06	29 13		08 01		05 19	33	18 54	
07	29 16		08 11		04 41		19 09	
08	29 19		08 21		04 02	34	19 23	
09	29 22		08 31		03 22		19 38	
10	29 25		08 40		02 42	35	19 52	
11	29 29		08 49		02 00		20 06	
12	29 34		08 58		01 18		20 21	
13	29 38		09 07		00 35	36	20 35	
14	29 43		09 15		29 ♍ 52		20 50	
15	29 48		09 24		29 08		21 04	
16	29 54		09 32		28 24	37	21 19	
17	00 ♊ 00		09 40		27 39		21 33	
18	00 06		09 47		26 53		21 48	
19	00 12		09 55		26 08	38	22 03	
20	00 19		10 02		25 22		22 17	
21	00 25		10 09		24 35		22 32	
22	00 33		10 16		23 49	39	22 46	
23	00 40		10 22		23 02		23 01	
24	00 48	03	10 28		22 16		23 16	
25	00 56		10 34		21 29		23 30	16
26	01 04		10 40		20 43		23 45	
27	01 12		10 45		19 57		24 00	
28	01 21		10 50		19 10	40	24 14	
29	01 29		10 55		18 25		24 29	
00 ♈	01 39		11 00	03	17 39		24 44	

☉	⚷ NN	V	⚷ SN	V	⚸ NN	V	⚸ SN	V
12 ♒	07 ♎ 25	-15	09 ♓ 02	-12	28 ♓ 17	53	22 ♑ 33	25
13	07 09	-16	09 19		27 53		22 51	
14	06 52		09 36	-13	27 29	52	23 09	
15	06 35	-17	09 53		27 06		23 27	
16	06 17		10 10		26 44		23 45	
17	05 58		10 27		26 22	51	24 03	26
18	05 39	-18	10 44		26 01		24 21	
19	05 19		11 02		25 41	50	24 39	
20	04 59	-19	11 19		25 22		24 57	
21	04 38		11 37		25 04		25 14	
22	04 16	-20	11 54		24 46	49	25 32	
23	03 54		12 12	-14	24 29		25 50	
24	03 31	-21	12 29		24 12		26 07	
25	03 07		12 47		23 56	48	26 25	
26	02 43	-22	13 05		23 41		26 42	
27	02 18	-23	13 22		23 27	47	27 00	
28	01 53		13 40		23 13		27 17	
29	01 27	-24	13 58		23 01		27 34	
00 ♓	01 00		14 16		22 48	46	27 51	
01	00 33	-25	14 34		22 37		28 09	
02	00 06	-26	14 52		22 26	45	28 26	
03	29 ♍ 38		15 10	-15	22 15		28 43	27
04	29 09	-27	15 28		22 06		29 00	
05	28 40		15 46		21 57	44	29 16	
06	28 11	-28	16 04		21 48		29 33	
07	27 41	-29	16 22		21 40		29 50	
08	27 10		16 40		21 33	43	00 ♒ 06	
09	26 39	-30	16 58		21 26		00 23	
10	26 08	-31	17 16		21 20		00 39	
11	25 37		17 35		21 15	42	00 55	
12	25 05	-32	17 53	-16	21 10		01 12	
13	24 33	-33	18 11		21 05		01 28	
14	24 00		18 29		21 01	41	01 44	
15	23 28	-34	18 47		20 58		01 59	
16	22 55		19 06		20 55		02 15	28
17	22 22	-35	19 24		20 53	40	02 31	
18	21 49	-36	19 42		20 51		02 46	
19	21 16		20 01		20 49		03 02	
20	20 42	-37	20 19	-17	20 48	39	03 17	
21	20 09	-38	20 37		20 48		03 32	
22	19 36		20 56		20 48		03 47	
23	19 02	-39	21 14		20 49	38	04 02	
24	18 29		21 32		20 50		04 17	
25	17 56	-40	21 51		20 52		04 31	29
26	17 23		22 09		20 54		04 46	
27	16 50	-41	22 27		20 56	37	05 00	
28	16 17		22 46	-18	20 59		05 14	
29	15 44	-42	23 04		21 02		05 28	
00 ♈	15 12		23 22				05 42	

House/Planet/Sign Combinations

House	Planet	Sign	Element	Quality
1 (+)	♂ Mars	♈ Aries	Fire	Cardinal
2 (-)	♀ Venus	♉ Taurus	Earth	Fixed
3 (+)	☿ Mercury	♊ Gemini	Air	Mutable
4 (-)	☽ Moon	♋ Cancer	Water	Cardinal
5 (+)	☉ Sun	♌ Leo	Fire	Fixed
6 (-)	☿ Mercury	♍ Virgo	Earth	Mutable
7 (+)	♀ Venus	♎ Libra	Air	Cardinal
8 (-)	♀ Pluto	♏ Scorpio	Water	Fixed
9 (+)	♃ Jupiter	♐ Sagittarius	Fire	Mutable
10 (-)	♄ Saturn	♑ Capricorn	Earth	Cardinal
11 (+)	♒ Aquarius	♒ Aquarius	Air	Fixed
12 (-)	♆ Neptune	♓ Pisces	Water	Mutable

Each line shares the same key meaning, e.g., the first house, Mars, and Aries are cardinal fire and symbolize direct self-expression and self-will in action.

The use of the terms "positive" and "negative" in astrology is similar to their use in electricity, with no connotation of good and bad. Positive signs (air and fire) are active, open, spontaneous, and oriented to outward expression. Negative signs (earth and water) are reactive, concealing, deliberate, serious, and oriented to preservation and retention.

Although the three outer and more recently discovered planets have been assigned to rulership of three signs, the traditional rulers of these signs must still be taken into account in reading houses of the chart ruled by them. Thet are: Jupiter as co-ruler of Pisces; Saturn as co-ruler of Aquarius; and Mars as co-ruler of Scorpio. The four asteroids, between Mars and Jupiter, are proving valuable. Ceres and Vesta seem to share the rulership of Virgo with Mercury, while Pallas and Junno share the rulership of Libra with Venus.

Key Phrases for House/Planet/Sign Combinations

♈ Aries   ♂ Mars

Free self-expression; self-will in spontaneous action; initiative, impulse, courage, pioneering spirit, vitality, skilled coordination, enthusiasm for the new, ready to fight against any limits on personal freedom. "I do my thing."

♉ Taurus   ♀ Venus

Pleasure in manipulating the physical sense world; comfort, security, contentment, love of beauty in tangible possessions; deliberate, persisting determination, slow to become angry or forget. "I enjoy the sense world."

♊ Gemini   ☿ Mercury

Consciousness, capacity to learn and communicate; thought, language, contact with nearby equals, dexterity, curiosity, versatility, multiple interests, flexibility, cheerful, witty, flippant. "I see, conceptualize and talk."

♋ Cancer   ☽ Moon

The personal unconscious; memory; dependence or nurturance; absorption, protection, preservation, sensitivity, empathy, need for warmth and emotional closeness and rootedness. "I save, protect, nourish and assimilate."

♌ Leo   ☉ Sun

Ego-expansion and creativity; urge to transcend the past, to be in the limelight, to win admiration, applause, love; enthusiasm, joy, drama, leadership, magnetism, generosity, pride. "I rejoice in projecting my personal power into the world."

♍ Virgo   ☿ Mercury

Efficient functioning in one's job and in one's body; focus on flaws in order to correct them; service; productive work; analysis, discrimination, pragmatism, quiet efficiency, attention to detail; self-restraint, humility, interest in health and healing. "I work competently."

♎ Libra   ♀ Venus

Partnership, cooperation or competition with equals; justice, both sides in balance; harmony, arbitration, pleasure from grace, line, form, a feeling for space, and for interaction with peers; need for "equal others" to feel complete. "I enjoy balance."

♏ Scorpio ♀ Pluto

Self-knowledge learned through the mirror of a mate and self-mastery learned out of respect for the rights of the mate; ability to give, to receive, and to share for mutual satisfaction; passionate intensity; learning what is ours and what belongs to someone else, how to love and yet let go, when to stop, to discard the outgrown past. "I share the sense world with others for mutual pleasure and seek selfknowledge and self mastery."

♐ Sagittarius ♃ Jupiter

Search for the intellectual absolute, philosophical, religious and ethical belief systems; definition of what is real, true, morally right, and valuable, the basis for choices and goals; trust, optimism, humor, generosity, expansiveness; love of books, travel, nature, or sports, depending upon the definition of value; the urge to reach further. "I trust, value and direct my life according to my understanding."

♑ Capricorn ♄ Saturn

Law—karmic, natural, manmade—what we can do, what we can't do, what we must do; the nature of the world which sets the outer limits to self-will, and the conscience which sets inner limits; the Puritan virtues—duty, responsibility, thrift, practicality, realism; the need for power and achievement, either to feel secure from the world's threat, to attain a sense of self-worth, or to avoid guilt; crystallized structure from social institutions to bones and teeth. "I carry out the law."

♒ Aquarius ♅ Uranus

Voluntary community without coercion; everyone equalitarian, open, individualistic, accepting; the search for new knowledge; rebellion against tradition or any other limitation in order to facilitate growth; explosive struggle against routine or restriction. "I seek to expand knowledge and freedom for all humanity."

♓ Pisces ♆ Neptune

Search for emotional absolutes, for infinite love and beauty; the mystic who is one with the whole; sensitivity, empathy, compassion, creative imagination, fantasy, the artist, the savior, or the victim seeking an easy road to the great vision through drugs, alcohol, psychosis, or invalidism; moving toward the vision or waiting for the world to give it. "I dream of love and beauty and am absorbed in the whole."

Aspects

♂ Conjunction   Degrees Apart: 0°   Fraction of Circle: 0
Orb: 10-12°   Power: Very Strong
Nature: Depends on planets, sign and house involved and other aspects to the conjunction

⊻ Semi-sextile   Degrees Apart: 30°   Fraction of Circle: 1/12
Orb: 3°   Power: Weak
Nature: Potential harmony

∠ Semi-square   Degrees Apart: 45°   Fraction of Circle: 1/8
Orb: 5°   Power: Moderate
Nature: Friction

✳ Sextile   Degrees Apart: 60°   Fraction of Circle: 1/6
Orb: 7°   Power: Moderate
Nature: Harmony, Opportunity

□ Square   Degrees Apart: 90°   Fraction of Circle: 1/4
Orb: 8-10°   Power: Strong
Nature: Stress, Conflict

△ Trine   Degrees Apart: 120°   Fraction of Circle: 1/3
Orb: 8-10°   Power: Strong
Nature: Harmony, Talent

⟐ Sesqui-Square   Degrees Apart: 135°   Fraction of Circle: 3/8
Orb: 5°   Power: Moderate
Nature: Friction

⊼ Inconjunct   Degrees Apart: 150°   Fraction of Circle: 5/12
Orb: 3°   Power: Strong
Nature: Strain, Separation, Adjustment

☍ Opposition   Degrees Apart: 180°   Fraction of Circle: 1/2
Orb: 8-10°   Power: Strong
Nature: Separation or Cooperation

∥ Parallel   Degrees Apart: 0°, Same Declination
Orb: 1°   Power: Moderate
Nature: Similar to Weak Conjunction

⚸ Anti-Parallel   Degrees Apart: 0°, Opposite Declination
Orb: 1°   Power: Moderate
Nature: Similar to Weak Opposition

Minor Aspects

The following aspects developed by Kepler are based on a division of the circle by fifths. All are mildly harmonious with creative potentials. Orb is limited to 2° or less. Very weak unless exact.

Viginitile   Degrees Apart: 18°   Fraction of Circle: 1/20
Decile   Degrees Apart: 36°   Fraction of Circle: 1/10
Quintile   Degrees Apart: 72°   Fraction of Circle: 1/5
Tredecile   Degrees Apart: 108°   Fraction of Circle: 3/10
Biquintile   Degrees Apart: 144°   Fraction of Circle: 2/5

The following aspects are very weak aspects with a 1° orb, and are not in common use.

Undecagon   Degrees Apart: 33+°   Fraction of Circle: 1/11
Nonagon   Degrees Apart: 40°   Fraction of Circle: 1/9
Septile   Degrees Apart: 51+°   Fraction of Circle: 1/7

John Nelson's forecasts of ionospheric disturbances support aspects for every multiple of 7½, 11¼, and 18 degrees. The new aspects should be limited to a 1° orb and are probably only significant when involved in combinations with traditional aspects.

Harmonics   Degrees Apart: 7½, 11¼, 18

*Zip Dobyns receives the Lifetime Achievement Award from ISAR
(International Society for Astrological Research).*

Zipporah Pottenger Dobyns received her Ph.D. in clinical psychology and was also certified as a professional astrologer (1960) by the American Federation of Astrologers (and by International Society of Astrological Research when they developed a certification program). Zip was also a minister in the Community Church of Religious Science. She lectured and gave workshops all over the world and held many Astrological Intensives that lasted from 10 to 16 days—teaching astrology and psychology to students in Canada, Mexico, the United States, Australia, and New Zealand.

Zip won numerous astrological awards from her peers, including Best Lecturer (Virgo) at AFA many times, two Regulus Awards from ISAR (for Research and Innovation and for Teaching), the coveted Southern Cross from the Federation of Australian Astrologers, Outstanding Contribution to the Art & Science of Astrology from Professional Astrologers Incorporated, Service to Astrology from Aquarius Workshops, and the Lifetime Achievement Award from International Society from Astrological Research.

A prolific writer, Zip authored a number of books including (1977) *The Asteroid Ephemeris*; (1973) *Astrologer's Casebook* (with Nancy Roof); (1996) *The Book of Saturn*; (1972) *Distance Values*; (1972) *Evolution through the Zodiac;* (1983) *Expanding Astrology's Universe*; (1973) *Finding the Person in the Horoscope*; (2002) *Healing Mother/Daughter Relationships* (with Maritha Pottenger); (1973) *The Node Book*; (1994) *Planets on the Move* (with Maritha Pottenger); (1975) *Progressions, Directions and Rectification*; (1985) *Seven Paths to Understanding* (with William Wrobel); (1998) *Unveiling your Future* (with Maritha Pottenger); and (1977) *The Zodiac as a Key to History*. Her book of poetry (*God's World*) was published in 1957 and she was working on children's poems (unpublished) before her passing in the summer of 2003.

Zip contributed to numerous astrological (and some psychological) journals, including *The Mutable Dilemma* and *Asteroid World* (now available online through ccrsdodona.org) for which she wrote the majority of the articles for 25 years.

Zip had four children of her flesh, three of whom were active in the astrological world (and the fourth in healing). Many of her students considered Zip to be their spiritual mother, and asked to be in the family next lifetime. (She had a first-house Moon, strong Ceres and Mars in the fourth house, so was very nurturing and a mother figure to many.) She is deeply missed.